Politicizing Consumer Choice

T0326575

Christian Gunkel

Politicizing Consumer Choice
Ethical Dimensions of Consumerism
in the United States

Bibliographic Information published by the Deutsche Nationalbibliothek
The Deutsche Nationalbibliothek lists this publication in the Deutsche Nationalbibliografie; detailed bibliographic data is available in the internet at http://dnb.d-nb.de.

Library of Congress Cataloging-in-Publication Data
Gunkel, Christian, 1984-
  Politicizing consumer choice : ethical dimensions of consumerism in the United States / Christian Gunkel. -- 1 Edition.
     pages cm
  ISBN 978-3-631-65475-0
  1. Consumption (Economics)--United States. 2. Consumer profiling--United States. 3. Social change--United States. I. Title.
  HC79.C6G86 2014
  174'.4--dc23
                            2014040516

                        ISBN 978-3-631-65475-0 (Print)
                      E-ISBN 978-3-653-04706-6 (E-Book)
                       DOI 10.3726/978-3-653-04706-6
                            © Peter Lang GmbH
                  Internationaler Verlag der Wissenschaften
                          Frankfurt am Main 2015
                             All rights reserved.
               PL Academic Research is an Imprint of Peter Lang GmbH.

           Peter Lang – Frankfurt am Main · Bern · Bruxelles · New York ·
                          Oxford · Warszawa · Wien

              All parts of this publication are protected by copyright. Any
        utilisation outside the strict limits of the copyright law, without
              the permission of the publisher, is forbidden and liable to
             prosecution. This applies in particular to reproductions,
           translations, microfilming, and storage and processing in
                          electronic retrieval systems.

                 This publication has been peer reviewed.

                           www.peterlang.com

To my parents
Thomas and Anke Gunkel

Contents

Acknowledgements

I am grateful to a number of people for their advice and support. To begin with, I would particularly like to thank Professor Astrid Franke of the University of Tübingen for her support and for writing the foreword.

I would also like to thank my friends: Nils Wiegand for bearing me company in the library and during our coffee breaks, Jonas Gasthauer whom I could turn to with all sorts of theoretical questions, and Daniel Gietz for encouraging me to publish my thesis. I am also grateful to Ina Schreiber for her patience with me as the deadline came closer. And finally, I want to thank my parents for their support.

Foreword

By Astrid Franke

Boycotting Starbucks, buying Fair Trade products, being involved in the No Logo movement – are these genuinely political activities or rather private ethical consumer choices? Can they threaten a capitalist organization of the market or are they always already part of the market – perhaps even a new type of economic engine? Beyond the hopes and fears one may have vis-à-vis general developments of the political economy, there are important historical experiences and theoretical traditions behind these two possible stances towards consumerism. On the one hand, there is the American cultural memory of a boycott of British consumer products, most notably tea, as part of a political move towards independence: The so-called Boston Tea Party, just like Gandhi's boycott of British clothes or the Montgomery Bus Boycott are cases where the refusal to buy certain services or products can undoubtedly regarded as genuine political action. On the other hand, the decisions to buy 'organic' has sparked off new brands and product lines, new supermarkets, and new food chains – it is just as undoubtedly a decision that has led to a diversification of the market. While these consumer choices might be ethically motivated they might also satisfy a desire for distinction amongst consumers that can easily be exploited by marketing strategies. Here, the descendants of theoretical traditions in which the consumer is regarded as a victim of manipulation and/or deprived of choices – notably the Frankfurt School – would come to the fore and claim that consumption cannot be a site of resistance or be regarded as political action. Or was this, perhaps, possible once but is no longer?

The following inquiry takes a rather skeptical view towards many current forms of consumer activism but is nevertheless rejecting the view of the easily manipulated consumer without agency. It does so, first, by a theoretical discussion of the consumer as agent or 'dupe' and second, by a historical survey of political consumerism from the American Revolution to the present in order to show the changing preconditions of political consumerism. Thus, the consumer is conceptualized in a way that should overcome the dichotomies between private consumption and political action, social manipulation and free agency. Drawing, amongst others, on Georg Simmel, Thorstein Veblen, David Riesman, and particularly on the French sociologist Pierre Bourdieu and his concept of *Habitus*, consumption is regarded as socially oriented action. While, depending on the kind of product and the historical moment, sheer need may play a role, too, our choices as consumers might increasingly be regarded as forms of communication, signaling to others how we want to be seen, what groups we want to belong to an, more importantly even, who we do *not* want to be associated with. And the closer we get to our present moment in history, the less satisfying it is to identify that 'group' with traditional status or even class, measurable through income and assets.

Inevitably, the question arises to what extent Bourdieu's findings which are predominantly based on research in France, can be transferred to the U.S. – a country which historically lacks a nationally acknowledged cultural center and a clear dichotomy of high versus low culture. As becomes clear in the discussion, however, Bourdieu's emphasis on the desire for distinction as a driving force for social processes goes a long way in explaining contemporary consumer culture – particularly when it is seen as a continuous process of seeking non-conformity rather than as an effort to just distinguish oneself from the one status group below. One decisive step then is to think of the social space as not only structured vertically but horizontally as well, and to recognize how time is included in the model: whatever seems hip, cool or simply distinctive ceases to be so when too many people have caught up with it. Those in search for non-conformity will then move on to something else. While one may see the idea of "currency" by Grant McCracken or Douglas Holt's "lifestyle" as a modification of Bourdieu, one might also note that the dynamics thus described actually resemble the mechanisms in the field of art as described by Bourdieu in the field of cultural production: Every avant-garde tries to establish a new position in the field and to distinguish itself from others, and "to introduce difference is to produce time"; the more people strive for non-conformity, the faster, the more ephemeral the field appears to be.[1]

---

1 Pierre Bourdieu, *The Field of Cultural Production: Essays on Art and Literature*. Ed. Randal Johnson. New York: Columbia University Press, 106.

To what extent this model then captures consumerism at a particular historical moment and what this may entail can be seen in a survey of the historic roots of political consumerism from the American Revolution to Fordism in Chapter 3: Here, the experiences of the American Revolution, the beginnings of the women's movement and the successes of the Civil Rights Movement form a tradition that may still inspire confidence in today's citizens to choose a form of activism that is directed at the producers and vendors of goods. Yet, there is another aspect to consider in today's setup: Inasmuch the state took an active role in the market, foremost in the New Deal and its aftermath, the citizen-consumer could plausible act in a triangle between the state and the market. Ralph Nader, who may be seen as the paradigmatic example of the consumer activist would thus seek a genuinely political arena and lobby for consumer protection, his effort being crowned with the formation of the Consumer Product Safety Commission in 1972. But as the state increasingly withdrew its regulatory force from the market, traditional consumer advocates loose their counterparts. Without a genuine political forum and its concomitant activities such as lobbying, voting, or campaigning for legal changes, activists now attempt to turn their buying decisions themselves into political acts, facing corporations as directly as they can. Inasmuch as their buying decisions are inevitably acts of distinguishing themselves, however, the 'alternatives' they envision can easily be incorporated into the system, as the examples of Trader Joe's, Burt's Bees or Odwalla may easily demonstrate. Not surprisingly then, this book ends by noting how corporations "have discovered the benefits of corporate social responsibility," profound changes addressing issues of sustainability, human rights or labor conditions have been elusive so far. They demarcate, perhaps, the limits of the politics to be made through consumer choices and the need for another addressee.

Prof. Dr. Astrid Franke is professor of American Studies at the University of Tübingen, Germany.

1. Introduction

Things are in the saddle, and ride mankind.[1]
—Ralph Waldo Emerson

Emerson's words appear like a bleak prediction of America's materialist future, and indeed the "primacy of the market"[2] has come to preside over most parts of the social space in the United States today. A number of social theorists and consumer activists alike frequently regard this as a negative development. Although consumption has played a central role throughout American history, it was only in the twentieth century that one could start to speak of mass consumption. The rise of Fordism, which brought about a variety of technical innovations allowing for the mass production of consumer goods, would spawn an unforeseen amount of consumption. Eventually, the Fordist regime culminated in the mass consumerism of the post-World War II era. And in the 1950s, consumer culture proved to be a fertile ground for the emergent consumer critique of the Frankfurt School. In particular, Herbert Marcuse's theory of a totalitarian, one-dimensional society "[precluding] the emergence of an effective opposition" and in which individuals are "[...] kept incapable from being autonomous"[3] would find great response during the following years, especially in the 1960s. In contrast to the theories of the Frankfurt School, which conceptualize the consumer as dupe[4], there are theories of consumer sovereignty, which are closely related to the rise of liberalism.

---

1   Ralph Waldo Emerson, "Ode, Inscribed to W.H. Channing," in *The American Transcendentalists: Essential Writings*, ed. Lawrence Buell (New York: Modern Library, 2006), 460.
2   Matthew Hilton, "Consumers and the State Since the Second World War," *Annals of the American Academy of Political and Social Science* 611 (May 2007): 74.
3   Herbert Marcuse, *One-Dimensional Man: Studies in the Ideology of Advanced Industrial Society* (London: Routledge, 2002), 5, 8.
4   See: Juliet B. Schor, "In Defense of Consumer Critique: Revisiting the Consumption Debates of the Twentieth Century," *Annals of the American Academy of Political and Social Science* 611 (May 2007): 22.

Conceptualizing the consumer as a sovereign, active, and creative agent, these theories regard consumption as "[...] a private sphere which must be free from interference by external social authorities."[5] In other words, consumer sovereignty means that the individual is entirely free in their choices. However, as Juliet Schor argues, "the agents versus dupes framing has been a theoretical cul-de-sac."[6]

Yet there are strong indications that consumer agency plays a central role in modern consumer society and especially in ethical and political consumerism. For instance, the individual Pierre Bourdieu's conceptualizes in his theory of distinction shows a great deal of goal-directed action and self-determination. Thereby, he delivers a rather precise account of the general functioning of consumer society. Distinction, according to Bourdieu, is in essence a type of domination of one group over another based on the distribution of "cultural capital."[7] Even though his theory focuses on the upper class in France, some of his concepts may be adapted to the United States, as chapter two will show. Bourdieu's idea of the consumer as a social actor who orients his or her action towards other individuals is an important point to start with. Michel Foucault devises a similar notion wherein social action is basically the enactment of power relations that pervade society and not the result of a social superstructure that exerts influence over individuals. His idea of "action upon action"[8] describes an active form of reflected individual behavior. Especially with regard to postmodernism, in which the individual responds to other individuals rather than social authorities, theories which focus on individual social action seem to be the most suitable in an approach to consumer culture, as chapter two will elaborate.

---

5   Don Slater, *Consumer Culture and Modernity* (Cambridge, UK; Cambridge, MA: Polity Press; Blackwell Publishers, 1997), 35.
6   Schor, "In Defense of Consumer Critique," 24.
7   See: Pierre Bourdieu, *Distinction: A Social Critique of the Judgement of Taste* (London: Routledge, 2010), 225. For Bourdieu, cultural capital defines "dispositions and competences which are not distributed universally," but which are an essential precondition for "the appropriation of cultural goods."
8   Michel Foucault, "The Subject and Power," in *Michel Foucault: Beyond Structuralism and Hermeneutics*, by Hubert L. Dreyfus and Paul Rabinow (Chicago: The University of Chicago Press, 1982), 220.

Postmodernism, which is the cultural manifestation of neoliberalism, may be seen as the product of the sweeping social, cultural, political and economic changes that came with the demise of Fordism in the late 1960s, which was followed by a recession in the 1970s. The outcome was a fundamentally restructured market and society as the economic and political spheres became increasingly separated. This postmodern transition also spawned a new, different kind of consumer focused on the self and individuality, for whom buying "is only rarely a functional act."[9] Instead, as Grant McCracken holds, "[c]onsumer goods, in their anticipation, choice, purchase, and possession, [have become] an important source of the meanings with which we construct our lives."[10] Therefore, rather than Jean Baudrillard's idea of consumption as "permanent festive celebration of objects,"[11] consumption has indeed become a source of identity. But, at the same time, it is important to note that it is "[...] nearly impossible to construct identity outside the consumer marketplace."[12]

When it comes to the political and ethical dimensions of consumption, the use of approaches that focus on the consumer as agent is imperative. Yet what is potentially problematic, with regard to the use of consumer-as-agent-theories, is that alternative consumption combines two spheres which are traditionally separated in most theories on consumption – the public and the private. This results in a dichotomy between collective and individual forms of action; whereas the former is generally seen as located in the public sphere of politics, consumption is commonly regarded as a form of action undertaken individually and in private.

9   Bryant Simon, "Not Going to Starbucks: Boycotts and the Out-Sourcing of Politics in the Branded World," *Journal of Consumer Culture* 11, no. 2 (July 2011): 163.
10 Grant McCracken, *Culture and Consumption II: Markets, Meaning, and Brand Management* (Bloomington: Indiana University Press, 2005), 164.
11 Jean Baudrillard, "Consumer Society," in *Consumer Society in American History: A Reader*, ed. Lawrence Glickman (Ithaca NY: Cornell University Press, 1999), 33.
12 Schor, "In Defense of Consumer Critique," 25.

Regarding the long history of consumer politics in the United States, this differentiation may not be upheld, as this work intends to demonstrate. As Davan Shah et al. argue, some historians argue that "[…] consumer politics shaped the American Revolution and laid the groundwork for nationhood."[13] And, as a matter of fact, one will find that even in pre-industrial America market-based action were used as means to political ends, which will be shown in chapter three. However, whereas consumer politics had close ties to formal government policy, more often than not, well beyond the mid-twentieth century, neoliberalism has brought forth a new kind of consumer movement whose primary sphere of activity is the market. Earlier consumer movements advocated consumer interests, with regard to corporations as well as the government, and aimed at influencing the legislative process. However, as the state retreated from the market, consumer activists increasingly turned towards the informal politics of the market.

Today's consumer activism, or political consumerism, which has its roots in the counterculture of the 1960s, is largely the product of neoliberal globalization. Its range of issues extends beyond mere aspects of production and consumption and into the spheres of environmentalism, corporate politics and ethics. Especially during the 1990s, which are generally considered the heyday of consumer activism, consumer activist groups increasingly targeted multinational corporations and brands. Starbucks and Nike have been among the most prominent targets since then. These and other companies have been repeatedly attacked for issues like exploitive methods of production in third world countries or for lack of sustainability. Undoubtedly, the consumerist landscape in America has undergone certain changes since then as corporations increasingly began to see consumers as a force to reckon with. But despite the fact that a subversive potential is oftentimes ascribed to some consumer movements, not uncommonly by the activists themselves, consumer capitalism is still in

---

13 Davan V. Shah et al., "Political Consumerism: How Communication and Consumption Orientations Drive 'Lifestyle Politics'," *Annals of the American Academy of Political and Social Science* 611 (May 2007): 217.

place and far from being threatened by subversion or even a 'revolution.' Instead, sweatshop-free and fair-trade products have found their niche in the vast array of consumer goods. The authors of *Nation of Rebels*, Joseph Heath and Andrew Potter, even claim that "[...] cultural rebellion [read 'rebel consumerism'] [...] is not a threat to the system – it is the system."[14] With this in mind, one must note that alternative consumerism takes place, for the most part, within the boundaries of the market. Therefore, one must regard political and ethical consumerism not as the opposite of consumerism but rather as one specific peculiarity thereof, as chapter four will illustrate.

The central hypothesis of this work is that, by and large, alternative consumption follows the same rules as consumption in general. And this raises the question of whether, and to what extent, consumption may be regarded to have public and political implications, instead of being a merely private act. As recent research suggests, political and ethical consumption "[...] might be a new form of civic engagement,"[15] which means that the concepts of the consumer and the citizen should not be regarded as mutually exclusive. Hence, one of the central questions is if and to what degree consumer choice is free, or, rather, to what extent may consumer choice be considered a political decision. Of course, this entails an investigation of the limits of consumer agency, which will be dealt with in chapter two. Therefore, it is necessary to subject the consumer to closer theoretical scrutiny. The focus of chapter three is on political dimensions of consumption and consumer activism from a historical perspective, and ultimately concludes with a look at the postmodern condition of consumption. The latter may be regarded, to a certain extent, as the cradle of contemporary forms of consumer activism and alternative consumption, which will be examined in chapter four. Furthermore, in light of the question of whether alternative consumption

---

14 Joseph Heath and Andrew Potter, *Nation of Rebels: Why Counterculture Became Consumer Culture*. (New York: HarperBusiness, 2004), 1.
15 Michelle Nelson, Mark A. Rademacher, and Hye-Jin Paek, "Downshifting Consumer = Upshifting Citizen? An Examination of a Local Freecycle Community," *Annals of the American Academy of Political and Social Science* 611 (May 2007): 142.

is elitist or democratic,[16] the role cultural capital and distinction may play in alternative consumption will also be discussed. Above all, the overriding question will be: To what extent can consumer activist movements, and alternative consumerism in general, ultimately be considered an affirmation of neoliberal segmentation of the market rather than a subversive force?

---

16 See: Dietlind Stolle, Marc Hooghe, and Michele Micheletti, "Politics in the Supermarket: Political Consumerism as a Form of Political Participation," *International Political Science Review* 26, no. 3 (July 2005): 258.

2. Theorizing the Consumer

2.1 A Theoretical Outline of Alternative Consumption

Delivering an irrefutable definition of alternative consumption, ethical and political consumption that is, turns out to be a rather intricate undertaking. Furthermore, the fact that both terms are sometimes used conterminously does not seem to facilitate a solution to this problem. Generally speaking, ethical consumption can be described as consumer decisions based on the simple distinction between 'right' and 'wrong', or, in other words, actions made in accordance with a belief in doing the right thing. Political consumption, on the other hand, may also be based on similar ethical considerations, but also aims at more wide-ranging ends that reach into the public realm and might even have an impact on the collective. In contrast, ethical consumption, although not exclusively, may be seen as an individual form of consumption which is also very likely to take place in the private realm. Thus, despite the commonalities, it is helpful to differentiate between political and ethical consumption, as well as political and ethical consumerism. Hence, in this work, political consumerism is regarded as an extension of ethical consumerism.

Whether it be the anti-sweatshop movement, the fair trade movement, green consumerism, or campaigns for organic food, despite the profound differences in purpose, each movement carries a specific ethical meaning and more often than not a political meaning as well. Regardless of the etymological implications of these terms, namely that political consumerism – not just etymologically but also historically – implies some form of collective action whereas ethical consumerism does not necessarily, the question arises whether, and under what circumstances, this differentiation can be maintained. Dietlind Stolle and Marc Hooghe describe political consumerism as "[l]oose, non-bureaucratic, individualized action,"[1] but this is nowhere near sufficient as description, for 'ethical consumerism'

---

1 Dietlind Stolle and Marc Hooghe, "Consumers as Political Participants?" in *Politics, Products, and Markets: Exploring Political Consumerism Past and Present*, ed. Michele Micheletti, Andreas Follesdal, and Dietlind Stolle (New Brunswick, NJ: Transaction Publishers, 2009), 273.

could be defined with the exact same words. Also, this definition does not manage to resolve the collective vs. individual dichotomy. Furthermore the authors state that political consumers "[...] consider the market as an arena for politics and ethical action [...]."[2] In a sense, this insinuates that there may be only a thin line between political and ethical consumerism if there is one at all.

Especially with respect to ethical consumerism, making a distinction between political and ethical consumerism is complicated as they are closely intertwined and sometimes even appear to coincide with each other. Thus, clearly, both are connected in some way, and, in any case, it is virtually impossible to discern a division between the two. According to Michele Micheletti, ethical consumerism must be considered as merely one specific among several peculiarities of political consumerism, which includes "[...] consumer activism, ethical consumption, and socially responsible investing."[3] She develops the term 'political consumerism' as a sort of umbrella term subsuming all the other forms of consumer activism. And, indeed, most forms of alternative consumption convey strong political implications. Even though Micheletti's truly insightful work convincingly argues how ethical consumption is merely a form of political consumption, it is nevertheless helpful to distinguish between different forms of alternative consumerism. In the following the terms shall therefore be treated as equal but not exactly coterminous.

As already suggested, defining alternative consumerism as merely the opposite of consumerism leads only to a theoretical dead-end. Instead, it makes much more sense to conceive of political and ethical consumerism as a specific form of consumerism itself. At the very least, one should acknowledge that both are founded on the same basic principles of the marketplace. Hence, it is useful to include theories of conventional consumerism in a prolific approach to political and ethical consumerism. However, this is aggravated by the fact that political consumerism combines two aspects which some theorists regard as most contradictory – politics and consumption. Even though this aspect should not be neglected, politics and consumerism must not be regarded as mutually

---

2 Stolle and Hooghe, "Consumers as Political Participants?" 273.
3 Michele Micheletti, *Political Virtue and Shopping: Individuals, Consumerism, and Collective Action* (Basingstoke, UK: Palgrave Macmillan, 2010), 2.

exclusive; instead the question of whether, and to what degree, consumption may be seen as a political act must be solved. Contradictory to common sense, which clearly differentiates between individual and collective action, the idea of politicized consumer choice implies an individual action with a potentially collective outcome. This makes it a special case and all the more interesting as a subject for closer scrutiny.

2.1.1 'Ordinary' and Alternative Consumption

It is important to note that, just as "[c]onsumerism is not coterminous with consumption,"[4] one must not confuse political consumerism with political consumption. Despite both being inseparably connected, there is a fundamental difference, namely that "[...] consumerism is the cultural expression and manifestation of the apparently ubiquitous act of consumption."[5] It is fair to say that the same applies to the relation between political consumerism and political consumption as well. Indeed, underlying both political consumerism and consumerism in general is the fact that each is a manifestation of certain acts of consumption. Furthermore, Miles suggests that consumerism may very well have a "social and ideological impact."[6] This is an essential implication particularly with regard to political and ethical consumerism because it allows for the use of traditional theories of consumerism and consumption in an approach to alternative consumerism and consumption. This presumption is in fact reinforced by the key finding of Clive Barnett et al., which is that "[...] there is no *necessary* implication that 'ethical consumption' implies less consumption, quite the reverse."[7] Hence it is safe to assume that the same, or at least similar, basic principles of consumerism also hold true for political and ethical consumerism.

---

4   Steven Miles, *Consumerism: As a Way of Life* (London; Thousand Oaks, CA: Sage Publications, 1998), 3.
5   Ibid., 4.
6   Ibid.
7   Clive Barnett, Philip Cafaro, and Terry Newholm, "Philosophy and Ethical Consumption," in *The Ethical Consumer*, ed. Rob Harrison, Terry Newholm, and Deirdre Shaw (London: Sage, 2005), 21.

Political consumerism may be seen as spanning both the private realm of consumption and the public realm of politics, with the private being the individual and the public being the domain of the collectivity. Perhaps politics and consumption are not such a contradictory pairing after all, for, in both fields, there are discernible forms of activism which at times even stretch beyond their scope. Both may involve certain forms of protest that "[...] may be directed against governments or against companies."[8] However, the peculiarity of consumption, and especially political consumption, is that the nature of this sort of action can be both individual as well as collective. At times, notably, it exhibits both characteristics at once. An individual act or decision always underlies a collective act, as for example in boycotts. Thus, the normative morality of a given society, or a group of people within that society, is not the only guiding principle to which acts of any kind of consumption are aligned. Individual moral convictions are, at least, equally important, especially with regard to alternative consumption. In fact, as Barnett et al. have found, "[...] the basis for an ethical consumption is to be found in the morality of ordinary consumption."[9] This is an important indication that neither political nor ethical consumerism should be understood as detached from ordinary consumerism.

In other words, to allocate ethical consumer behavior exclusively to the realm of alternative consumerism obscures the fact that even most commonplace acts of consumption may involve certain moral concerns. Indeed, consumer decisions and acts of purchasing often involve a comparably great deal of ethical considerations. As Colin Campbell observes, "[...] the idea that decisions [made by consumers] might involve a clear ethical or moral dimension is hardly new."[10] He refers to a survey on 1950s urbanite shoppers in Chicago conducted by Gregory P. Stone that already

---

8 Andreas Follesdal, "Political Consumerism as Chance and Challenge," in *Politics, Products, and Markets: Exploring Political Consumerism Past and Present*, ed. Michele Micheletti, Andreas Follesdal, and Dietlind Stolle (New Brunswick, NJ: Transaction Publishers, 2009), 8.

9 Barnett, Cafaro, and Newholm, "Philosophy and Ethical Consumption," 21.

10 Colin Campbell, "Considering Others and Satisfying the Self: The Moral and Ethical Dimension of Modern Consumption," in *The Moralization of the Markets*, ed. Nico Stehr, Christoph Henning, and Bernd Weiler (New Brunswick, NJ: Transaction Publishers, 2006), 221.

features a notion of ethical consumers. This is not just an early example of how closely ethics and consumption are connected, especially with regard to consumers – in this case housewives – preferring local shops to large department stores, it also states that "relatively high social status" is among the "[...] prime requisites for the development of an ethical orientation to the market."[11] This already implies that ethical purchase behavior is reserved for the more affluent, those whose consumer behaviors are not directed at satisfying merely the most basic needs. Furthermore, it also suggests that ordinary consumerism, which is based on wants or desires rather than needs, is a fertile ground for ethical and eventually political consumerism. Even with a more broadly defined consumer role – consumption is no longer confined to just the realm of housewives – this is more pertinent today than in the American consumer society of the 1950s. As a matter of fact, Colin Campbell observes that "[...] a want-based consumerism extends rather than decreases the role that ethics play in the conduct of consumers."[12]

The objectives and issues of ethical consumer behavior have changed dramatically. Whereas in the 1950s ethical concern was predominantly directed towards local community issues and individual health and well-being, nowadays the issues have become far more global. Today, ethical consumer decisions involve more than considerations about where and what to buy in order to support some local grocery store. Along with consumerism in general, ethical consumerism has expanded considerably, and, additionally, a substantial political dimension, reaching much farther than what Stone described, has become an essential element of the consumerist landscape in America. Thus the ethical and moral dimensions of ordinary consumption and consumerism alike can be regarded as a vital precondition for political consumerism to emerge.

At this point the primary question is not how ethics or politics are related to consumption, for this is rather easily detectable, but how the discrepancy between consumption as a private act and politics as a form

---

11 Gregory P. Stone, "City Shoppers and Urban Identification: Observations on the Social Psychology of City Life," *American Journal of Sociology* 60, no. 1 (July 1954): 43.
12 Campbell, "Considering Others and Satisfying the Self," 223.

of collective action can be reconciled in order to develop an approach to political consumerism. In a sense, there is still a theoretical gap between 'ordinary consumption' and 'political consumption', for, as mentioned above, the dichotomy between individual and collective forms of action still cannot be entirely reconciled. Thus, the introduction of the term ethical consumption or ethical consumerism appears rather conclusive, because ethics may encompass both the individual and the collective nature of acts of political consumption. Consequently, it appears reasonable to speak of ethical consumption as a link between the individual and the collective. Yet there is a difference between theory and practice since there is hardly a discernible boundary to be observed in actual consumer society that sets the different forms of consumption and consumer activism apart from each other. Rather, the boundaries between the different kinds of consumption are constantly in flux. In fact, one might well observe that the different spheres are at times overlapping or even merging and thus appear to be one and the same.

Over the decades, consumerism has become *the* dominant structuring principle of social life in the United States. As noted earlier, various ethical and moral motives may be found in acts of everyday consumption. Because consumerism comprises large proportions of the everyday lives of Americans, it is thus the logical point of departure for a conclusive approach to alternative consumerism. For, as Bertell Ollman critically claims:

> With the explosive expansion of consumerism – of the amount of time, thought, and emotions spent in buying and selling, and in preparing for (including worrying about) and recovering from these activities – the market has become a dominant, if not the dominant, influence in how people act and think throughout the rest of their lives.[13]

Similarly, Steven Miles argues that it was especially in the late twentieth century "[...] that consumption came to play a fundamentally formative social role in modern societies, and that we can begin to talk about

---

13 Bertell Ollman, "Market Mystification in Capitalism and Market Socialist Societies," in *Market Socialism*, ed. Bertell Ollman (New York: Routledge, 1998), 82, quoted in: Rob Harrison, Terry Newholm, and Deirdre Shaw, *The Ethical Consumer* (London: Sage, 2005), 4.

consumerism as a way of life."[14] But even earlier, in the 1950s, the American social critic Vance Packard similarly argued that "[...] Americans are co-operating wholeheartedly in the task of ever-greater consumption as a way of life."[15] And this is exactly the very context in which one has to approach political consumerism, namely as a particular outcome of this way of life.

Since consumerism and political consumerism are grounded on similar, or even the same, preconditions, both can be approached with similar theoretical instruments. The same social space with the same structures is the basis for all forms of consumption and consumerism being the socio-cultural context thereof. Thus, the basic assumption behind considering political consumption as a form of political participation[16] has to be that the consumer is able to act with self-determination, at least to some extent, and this form of self-determined action, is found in ordinary consumption. No matter that some acts of consumption are more individually motivated, whereas others are more public spirited;[17] in any case, some kind of self-determined individual action can be considered to underlie consumption. However, this does not necessarily imply that the consumer acts entirely autonomously, rather this is to imply that certain theories, especially those critical of consumerism – like Marcuse's, tend to underestimate the potential of the consumer as actor. Of course, this is not to say that theories critical of consumer culture have no right to exist, quite the contrary. Consumer critique, in many cases, is a vital element of the discourse of consumerism. The difficulty with Marcuse's theory is that it is not primarily devised to serve as an analytical instrument to study consumerism. Rather, and this is the core problem of this kind of critique, it merely identifies certain issues instead of delivering analytical explanations. Thus, an elaborate approach must be built upon solid theories that acknowledge the consuming individual as actor, and not as a marionette of consumer capitalism. Given the great deal of activity that takes place in the field of consumerism,

---

14 Miles, *Consumerism*, 10.
15 Vance Packard, *The Waste Makers* (Brooklyn: ig Publishing, 2011), 235.
16 See: Stolle, Hooghe, and Micheletti, "Politics in the Supermarket," 249.
17 See: Michael Schudson, "Citizens, Consumers, and the Good Society," *Annals of the American Academy of Political and Social Science* 611 (May 2007): 247.

it is quite futile to base one's approach on theories that regard the consumer as a passive and manipulated being. Yet one cannot deny that in countless situations the consumer's decisions may indeed be manipulated. There is no doubt that "[f]irms can and do persuade and manipulate consumers,"[18] but the idea that the consumer is entirely controlled by external forces and exists only at the will of the consumer industry remains utterly questionable.

2.1.2 Consumer Reflexivity and Decision-Making

Conceptualizing the consumer as an active and reflective being is therefore absolutely essential to gaining insight into political and ethical consumerism. Especially when examining individual and collective modes of consumer action, which do not necessarily involve an act of consumption but still have a consumerist objective, it is important to emphasize that the consumer's decision to participate is very likely based on reflected consideration rather than on manipulation. In this context, conventional boycotts directed at certain manufacturers or retailers, as well as the subcultural phenomenon of culture jamming[19], which will be discussed in chapter four, are among the most noteworthy forms of contemporary consumer activism. Even though no act of consumption is carried out, these actions can be understood as a deliberate consumer choice – the choice to not to buy certain goods for ethical and/or political reasons. In other words, deliberate non-consumption may also be regarded as a specific form of consumer behavior.

Thus, the decision to buy or not to buy a certain product or service follows largely the same pattern as ordinary consumption, but ethical and political considerations play a bigger role in the process of decision-making underlying consumer choice. What makes consumer choice political is not primarily the decision to not buy a specific good, but instead the

---

18 Roger A. Dickinson and Mary L. Carsky, "The Consumer as Economic Voter," in *The Ethical Consumer*, ed. Rob Harrison, Terry Newholm, and Deirdre Shaw (London: Sage, 2005), 29.
19 Culture jamming, one of the more prominent forms of consumer activism in sub-cultures, primarily targets at the alteration of advertising messages and brand images, and typically anti-capitalist vocabulary is used to promote anti-consumerism.

underlying intention which is made in a particular social context, and because alternative consumption does not necessarily imply less consumption, it is very likely that only a shift in consumption takes place. Products that are deemed bad are replaced by other goods that are more estimable in terms of mode of production and place of origin. Thus, more often than not, boycotting certain products for ethical or political reasons simply means buying one product instead of another – which is the essence of ethical consumerism, also called positive buying or simply buycotting.[20] Of course, there are also such phenomena as the voluntary simplicity movement or freecycle communities[21] which indeed involve less consumption – at least in terms of ordinary consumption behavior – but nevertheless sprang from the same motivations. This, however, is a rather marginal phenomenon in comparison to what is commonly called ethical or political consumerism. Hence, such movements, located outside the market, are of less significance to this analysis of the ethical and political dimensions of consumerism than those which are located within the sphere of the market. The bottom line remains: intentional choice paired with the firm belief to do the right thing underlies all of the above-mentioned forms of action.

In any case, and especially in the field of alternative consumerism, it is rather difficult to clearly distinguish between forms of consumption that expand to a collective setting and others that are rooted in the individual sphere. In fact, ethically and politically motivated consumer behavior may be seen as oscillating between both of these poles. At any rate, certain purposive consumer-related actions are involved that do not necessarily take place in the context of collectivity, and which might be more individually motivated. Nonetheless they are predicated on some kind of consumer choice – even if no explicit act of consumption is involved, as for example in the culture jamming movement. Despite the subversive character of such movements, what has happened so far is far from a profound revolution of the consumer marketplace; rather it seems one should speak of a mere

---

20 See: Scott Clouder and Rob Harrison, "The Effectiveness of Ethical Consumer Behaviour," in *The Ethical Consumer*, ed. Rob Harrison, Terry Newholm, and Deirdre Shaw (London; Thousand Oaks, CA: Sage, 2005), 96.
21 See: Nelson, Rademacher, and Paek, "Downshifting Consumer = Upshifting Citizen?" 142f.

'moralization of consumption,' and the outcome is what is commonly referred to as ethical or political consumerism. Although one cannot deny that changes have taken place, to approach these changes, one must first put them in their consumerist context.

2.2 The Myth of the Passive Consumer – The Consumer as Social Actor

To say that consumer choice can be political presupposes some notion of the consumer as an active individual. Even though, since the 1950s, a variety of theories have put strong emphasis on the image of the consumer as manipulated being, there are many reasons to assume that the capabilities of the consumer as social actor have oftentimes been underestimated. Nevertheless, some contemporary theorists seem to be highly doubtful of autonomously acting consumers. Indeed, consumers cannot be regarded as entirely autonomous actors, yet they cannot be seen as merely manipulated beings either. More often than not, both characteristics pertain to the role of the consumer. The consumer can very well be the passive and manipulated being, as many critics have argued, but at the same time – and here is the difficulty – the consumer can and has to also be described as an active and reflective being. Certainly, one cannot assume that this means the consumer is at all times aware of being manipulated, and it surely does not mean that consumer choice is solely directed by the manipulative powers of the advertising industry and large corporations. Much more, it can be regarded as interplay of both forces, the individual choices that are made, on the one hand, and the manipulative forces the consumer is exposed to, on the other.

2.2.1 The Private-Public-Dichotomy – Consumption and Political Action

One of the core problems in approaching alternative consumption lies in the fact that it combines two aspects, which are commonly regarded as mutually exclusive. Considerable fractions of 'traditional' consumer theory regard consumption and political action not just as entirely opposite forms of action, but also as taking place in different sectors of the social space. Consumption involves a great deal of individually motivated action, whereas, to a certain degree, political action entails a collective mode. Thus, conventional theorists have frequently dismissed the often-discussed opposition of the individual on the one hand, and the collective or public on the other, as irresolvable. One of the most outspoken theorists maintaining this contradistinction is Don Slater, a theorist who is a declared advocate of consumption as an exclusively individual form of action. He argues that "consumer choice is a private act," for "[...] it occurs within the domain of the private – of the individual, the household, the group of friends – which is ideologically declared out of bounds to public intervention." He continues, "[any] particular act of consumption is private in the sense of having no public significance."[22] Taking up on this idea of a strict confinement of consumption to the private, the only logical conclusion would be that consumption cannot be of any political significance at all, for politics obviously belong to the public realm. This highly individualistic and highly questionable perspective is only useful to a very limited extend, for it strictly denies that consumer action might have any effect other than "[increasing] private pleasures and comforts."[23] Thereby, the freedom of consumer choice or consumer sovereignty becomes confined to a narrow space and the dichotomy between the individual and the collective becomes an almost insurmountable obstacle, at least in.

Representing the exact opposite point of view, Michael Schudson, claims that "consumer decisions can be political."[24] He thereby ascribes to the consumer a certain discretionary potential, that underlies consumer action, and which allows for certain forms of action or choice that have an outcome other than just the fulfillment of private and individual interests. Schudson delivers a more powerful statement still by asserting that "political choices and consumer choices are [...] the same,"[25] and he does so by equating the consumer with the citizen. While there is certainly some truth to this daring proposition, it does not provide a solid basis for an examination of

---

22 Slater, *Consumer Culture and Modernity*, 28.
23 Ibid.
24 Schudson, "Citizens, Consumers, and the Good Society," 240.
25 Michael Schudson, "The Troubling Equivalence of Citizen and Consumer," *Annals of the American Academy of Political and Social Science* 608 (November 2006): 202.

alternative consumerism. The huge discrepancy between these two polariz-ing approaches is remarkable for they posit two extreme prospects on the same topic, and thus delimit the theoretical frame in which a fruitful anal-ysis can actually take place. Slater's concept precludes all kinds of public-spirited, and thus political, consumer action and stands in stark contrast to Schudson's approach, and yet, both are far from being an ideal tool to approach the political potential of consumer behavior. Schudson's view, however, appears to be the preferable, for his ideas correspond, to a certain extent, with Norbert Elias, who warns against conceptualizing the individual as mere opposite of society.[26]

Now, in order to develop a theoretical approach to consumer activism, a necessary premise is to gain an understanding of consumer behavior, because political and ethical consumption in turn is essentially a form of consumer behavior that manifests itself in the choices consumers of this particular group make. While one must not make the mistake of reduc-ing alternative consumption to the individual level of consumer action, as Schudson[27] rightly suggests to his readers, one should take individually motivated consumer actions or choices into consideration only insofar as they are the underlying precondition that enables the consumer to also act politically. Individual modes of action must be examined before con-tinuing with forms of collective action, which can be found in consumer activism.

2.2.2 The Relationship between the Individual and Consumer Society

The way in which the individual consumer relates to the collectivity of other consumers is especially important because the action that is involved is not merely self-referred. Interestingly, the individual-as-actor in fact orients a good deal of his action towards his or her social environment. In this context the celebrated Anglo-Polish social theorist Zygmunt Bauman puts special emphasis on individuality by stating that "[the] consumerist

---

26 See: Norbert Elias, *Die Gesellschaft der Individuen* (Frankfurt am Main: Suhrkamp, 1991), 210.
27 See: Schudson, "Citizens, Consumers, and the Good Society," 241.

vocation ultimately rests on individual performances." But, even more importantly, he further argues that "'[to] consume' therefore means to invest in one's own social membership [...]."[28] By describing society as a marketplace, he creates a highly individualized image of the social space, in which the actors basically act as individuals first and as collective second. And yet he acknowledges that individual behavior is by no means detached from the collective. But even before Bauman, in *The Lonely Crowd*, David Riesman tellingly described how the individual consumer relates to the group. His theory of the other-directed person focuses on the consumer's relationship to his particular peer-group, and how this relationship impacts the "socialization of consumption"[29] and eventually consumer behavior. His finding that "the membership [in a specific group] is engaged in *consuming* itself"[30] can be considered groundbreaking for many subsequent theories of consumerism, especially in view of Bauman's concept. In fact, even with five decades between them, both Riesman and Bauman recognize the competitiveness of consumption and identify the 'peer group' or "reference group"[31] as its driving force.

To some extent, Riesman's conception of 'other-direction' is still useful today, but one must bear in mind that it was based on entirely different premises than it would be today. During the 1950s, when *The Lonely Crowd* was written, middle class America had "[...] become a place of puritanical conformity and empty consumerism."[32] At least it was perceived this way by the rebellious youth and the emergent countercultural critique in particular, and also by many critics of consumer capitalism in general. On the other hand, the post-World-War-II-era was also seen as a time of upward mobility for large parts of the American society – the time when the proverbial 'Keeping up with the Joneses' was heavier with meaning than ever before. An expanding economy, the consequently rising standard of living, and manifold newly

---

28 Zygmunt Bauman, *Consuming Life* (Cambridge, UK: Polity Press, 2007), 55, 56.
29 David Riesman, Nathan Glazer, and Reuel Denney, *The Lonely Crowd: A study of the Changing American Character*, Reprint (New Haven, CT: Yale University Press, 2001), 81.
30 Ibid.
31 Bauman, *Consuming Life*, 82.
32 Thomas Frank, *The Conquest of Cool: Business Culture, Counterculture, and the Rise of Hip Consumerism*. (Chicago: University of Chicago Press, 1998), 7.

available options – especially in the realm of consumption – contributed to the rise of consumerism in the United States.[33] And this is exactly the setting for Riesman's 'other-direction' being "the dominant mode of insuring conformity"[34], which was the dominant theme of social criticism in America from the post-war era to the late 1960s. Thus, what David Potter identified as "the American's excessive concern with conformity"[35] in 1954 could also be interpreted as concern with keeping up with fellow consumers. However, even though conformity was the eventual outcome, it must not necessarily be regarded as what consumers primarily aspired to.

Certainly, other-directedness may be understood as analogous to Marcuse's 'one-dimensional man', who, living in a repressive society, is virtually incapable of any autonomous action.[36] However, with regard to the actual design of Riesman's concept, this understanding is not entirely accurate. Despite his critical tone, Riesman sees the consumer more as a social actor than as a suppressed and manipulated tool of the advertising industry. Following Marcuse, one could of course argue that this is exactly the kind of manipulation described in *One-Dimensional Man,* bereaving the individual of all options. However, an argumentation based on Marcuse might be accurate only if the totalitarian image of consumer society is understood as simply being the totality of the consumerist realm in which every action takes place. Being the dominant principle of structuring society, consumerism might very well be perceived as leaving no options, but in view of what has changed since then, one has to acknowledge that the consumer does indeed have certain options to choose from – although, admittedly these options are all within the scope of consumerism. And despite critics of consumerism would probably not agree, the fact that these options are clearly defined – yet infinitely changeable within this defined scope – is a necessary premise for the existence of society. Within this scope – or dimension – of consumption,

33 See: Grant McCracken, *Transformations: Identity Construction in Contemporary Culture* (Bloomington: Indiana University Press, 2008), 196.
34 Riesman, Glazer, and Denney, *The Lonely Crowd,* 20.
35 David M. Potter, *People of Plenty: Economic Abundance and the American Character* (Chicago: The University of Chicago Press, 1954), 49.
36 See: Marcuse, *One-Dimensional Man,* 79.

there is in fact a multitude of options to choose from and new options continually appear.

At this point, adopting a Foucauldian point of view is quite useful and, although one has to be careful about employing his ideas on consumer society par for par, it is nevertheless helpful in shedding some light on the mechanisms of society. One of Michel Foucault's central statements in *Discipline and Punish*, one that runs like a thread throughout almost all his work, is that the whole of society is steeped in all kinds of power relations. For him, 'power' is the structuring principle of society. Even though he leaves no doubt that there is no option to exist beyond the scope of power, he does not regard power as a negative thing per se. Rather, this sort of power – which must not be understood in the common way, as in the political power of states or governments, for instance – structures every kind of social relation. According to him, "[…] it is not that the beautiful totality of the individual is amputated, repressed, altered by our social order, it is rather that the individual is carefully fabricated in it […]."[37] This means the existence of such structuring principles is a constitutive and indispensable element of social life. This is also the exact antithesis to the approaches of the Frankfurt School of Critical Theory pioneered by Max Horkheimer and Theodor W. Adorno, and later also Herbert Marcuse.

Even more noteworthy is Foucault's argument that "[…] the principal elements are no longer the community and public life […]."[38] Thereby, Foucault stresses the role of the "private individual"[39] in contemporary society, which is especially relevant for the postmodern theories of consumption, which will be discussed below. Norbert Elias would later describe this development as the shift from the "we-identity" to the "I-identity"[40] in *Gesellschaft der Individuen*. According to Elias this change was the existential precondition for modern society and, furthermore, remarks

---

37 Michel Foucault, *Discipline and Punish: The Birth of the Prison*, trans. Alan Sheridan (London [etc.]: Penguin Books, 1991), 217.
38 Ibid., 216.
39 Ibid.
40 Elias, *Die Gesellschaft der Individuen*, 210; Norbert Elias, *The Society of Individuals*, trans. Michael Schröter (New York: Continuum, 2001), 156.

that "[...] the relation of individual and society [...] is not standing still."[41] To be more precise, it has to be seen as a process of constantly increasing complexity in the relation of individual and society, the outcome of which is ever-greater individualization.[42] Elias' discussion of the transition from tribal society to modern nation states implies that the individual is a product of this process. Accordingly, earlier forms of social organization that were based on rather small "survival units," a family or a tribe for instance, were thus dominated by a strong "we-identity." In other words, the group was the prime source of identity. In modern Western societies, however, these closely knit survival units have gradually been replaced by considerably larger survival units such as the state, and thus have lost their importance as reference groups. Consequently, 'we-identity' has become replaced by 'I-identity'.[43] With regard to the actual topic of this work, this is important insofar as this process towards a society with a highly complex division of labor may be regarded as a breeding ground for modern consumerism. Moreover, it is important to note that this shift more than likely induced not just a change of socialization, but also a change in the locus of social authorities.

The erosion of traditional 'survival units' – to use Elias' term – that comes with the advance of consumerism has also brought about a change in the socialization of the individual and the consumer respectively. In the context of consumerism, the family as a unit has lost its importance as structure of the individual's life, values, and source of identity. Instead, to revisit Riesman, various people, or groups of people, have replaced the family as the prime source of identity. Therefore, Riesman's concept of other-direction – in contrast to very family-oriented types of tradition-direction and inner-direction – can be seen as a methodical attempt to capture this development. The other-directed person represents the latest stage in the process of modes of socialization, starting with the stage of tradition direction. One of the most important findings articulated in *The Lonely Crowd* is that, in contrast to the other two types, "[...] the other-directed person learns to respond to signals from a far wider circle

---

41 Elias, *The Society of Individuals*, 162.
42 See: Ibid., 167f.
43 See: Ibid., 167, 178.

than is constituted by his parents,"[44] or social authorities that take on a form of parental role as in the case of inner-direction. Thus, the family is "[...] merely a part of a wider social environment to which he early becomes attentive."[45] However, Riesman also clarifies from the beginning that one mode does not replace the other, much more instead the different modes coexist in society.[46]

Although Riesman's approach may largely be seen as obsolete today, certain aspects of his concept of other-direction remain applicable. What makes his concept – at least in parts – still useful today is that, first of all, Riesman's 'other-directed man' is not conceptualized in the same way as Marcuse's 'one-dimensional man', who is essentially a manipulated and suppressed being condemned to passivity. Reading *The Lonely Crowd*, one will discover that passivity also plays a role in Riesman's approach, yet it is less a general condition than a possibility. Secondly, and even more importantly, Riesman, as already mentioned, puts strong emphasis on the peer group. He writes: "The frontiers for the other-directed man are people; he is people minded."[47] And this people-mindedness is exactly the angle from which one must view consumerism and hence political or ethical consumerism. This people-mindedness can also be translated into Norbert Elias' argument, namely that the individual and the society may not be seen as opposite.[48] Rather, the individual must be seen in relation to other individuals, and thus the group and eventually society. This circumstance, namely that humans are essentially and have always been social beings,[49] is vital to an approach to political and ethical consumerism. And even though Elias' approach to the interrelatedness of people is not exactly consumption related, it is ideally suited to this purpose, for only if the relation between the individual and the group, or more generally the society, is taken into account, will a fruitful approach to political consumerism be possible.

---

44 Riesman, Glazer, and Denney, *The Lonely Crowd*, 25.
45 Ibid.
46 See: Ibid., 32.
47 Ibid., 126.
48 See: Elias, *Die Gesellschaft der Individuen*, 9, 209, 246.
49 See: Ibid., 229.

Of course, the way the individual relates to the group has changed over the course of time and has become more complex than it was a hundred years ago. As Riesman assesses, the transition from inner-direction to other-direction was accompanied by an increasing complexity of the social environment within a few generations. Also, this was accompanied by a transition from a static to a more dynamic social environment. It is particularly interesting to note the striking similarities between this work and that of Norbert Elias describing the shift from 'we-identity' to 'I-identity', given the fact that some thirty years lie between both theories. However, Elias argues that the structure and dynamics of groups may be subject to rather quick changes, but, at the same time, that there are no regularities from which one could derive a universal principle to explain the social space.[50] This is as true today as it was in Riesman's days.

Another important aspect emphasized by Elias, and which is especially important for this consumerist approach, is that people seek orientation[51] or perhaps even some form of guidance,[52] and this can still be seen as vital with regard to contemporary consumerism. This means that there are certain authorities or groups of people that can be considered the forerunners whereas others merely follow the lead. In one form or another, this idea can be found in various works dealing with consumerism and consumption – since at least the turn of the century. For instance, Simmel's trickle-down theory, which would become one of the most influential theories on consumption, involves this idea to a certain extent. By setting a certain standard, the elite at the top of a given social hierarchy provides – albeit not intentionally –imitable models for the aspiring parties below, whose objective is to improve their social standing. The upper class thus has to turn towards new inventions in order to set itself apart from the subordinate classes, for, as McCracken remarks, "imitation provokes differentiation."[53] But there is another important aspect to

---

50 See: Elias, *Die Gesellschaft der Individuen*, 233.
51 See: Ibid., 234.
52 In the original German version of his book, Elias uses the term "Orientierung" which can be translated into both 'orientation' and 'guidance', however the latter carries stronger implications in terms of relations between humans. This in turn allows for a link to Riesman's theory.
53 McCracken, *Transformations*, 224.

the idea of imitation, namely the social dimension of this kind of action. Simmel described imitation as something "[...] which gives to the individual the satisfactions of not standing alone in his actions,"[54] and thereby gives weight to the interrelation of human beings, which is formative to most acts of consumption. Imitation – or emulation in Veblen's terms – requires the existence of a model or an authority, which grew from the prestige acquired by the elite by means of the "display of power and status."[55] Thereby, the elite – or "leisure class" as Veblen calls it – provides consumers with some kind of orientation, which, in turn, is the basis for this mechanism of imitation. Bourdieu, whose theory is based on a hierarchical model of society akin to Veblen and Simmel, uses the term "taste-maker"[56] to refer to the authority that determines what is legitimate taste and what is not. These 'taste-makers' can be seen as the ones whom other consumers orientate themselves towards.

Taste-makers are usually referred to as those groups of consumers who have the greatest say in the consumerist space. In traditional theory, these are the groups or elites standing at the top of status hierarchies. Most approaches based on a model of a static hierarchical society have fundamental shortcomings which make it impossible to use them one-to-one in political consumerism, because they neglect the role that alternative cultures or subcultures may play in the consumerist game. In other words, they are virtually incapable of apprehending changes that have not originated at the top of a status hierarchy. Of course, this is due to fact that when these theories were written the social order was fundamentally different from today. However, as Grant McCracken remarks, "[c]ertain innovations cannot be created by high status groups,"[57] therefore an approach is needed which is not based on a hierarchical model of society. Indeed, this aspect is crucial in view of contemporary consumer culture in America, especially with regard to political and ethical consumerism.

---

54 Georg Simmel, "Fashion," *American Journal of Sociology* 62, no. 6 (May 1957): 542.

55 John Storey, *Cultural Consumption and Everyday Life* (London: Arnold, 1999), 37.

56 Bourdieu, *Distinction*, 84.

57 McCracken, *Transformations*, 227.

Therefore, using Bourdieu's concept of distinction might at first appear to be equally problematic, because underlying his theory is the French society of the 1960s, which was still organized in a certain status hierarchy, and which was certainly more distinctly stratified than the American society of today.[58] But, despite this fact, what makes his theory applicable is its design. Bourdieu does not exclusively rely on objectively classifiable markers of class like e.g. economic positions. At least equally important to Bourdieu are subjective markers of class, such as taste. To mediate between both markers he develops the concept of habitus, which he describes as a "structured and structuring structure."[59] The habitus is structured by "different conditions of existence," such as education and economic position, and it structures (indirectly) the life-styles. As Bourdieu puts it:

> It is in the relationship between the two capacities which define the habitus, the capacity to produce classifiable practices and works, and the capacity to differentiate and appreciate these practices and products (taste), that the represented social world, i.e. the space of life-styles, is constituted.[60]

Since social status and life-styles do not merely derive from the objective economic position alone, but also include highly subjective or symbolic aspects such as taste, this approach, unlike others, is capable of grasping certain cultural peculiarities. Most important, however, is that "[as] a result of structuration, then, consumer tastes develop that are determined socially, not privately."[61] And this also explains the fact that political opinions may also be shaped by the habitus,[62] which makes this theory especially interesting with regard to political consumerism.

---

58 See: Lewis Friedland et al., "Capital, Consumption, Communication, and Citizenship: The Social Positioning of Taste and Civic Culture in the United States," *Annals of the American Academy of Political and Social Science* 611, no. 1 (May 2007): 33.

59 Bourdieu, *Distinction*, 167.

60 Ibid., 166.

61 A. Fuat Firat and Alladi Venkatesh, "Liberatory Postmodernism and the Reenchantment of Consumption," *The Journal of Consumer Research* 22, no. 3 (1995): 249.

62 See: Bourdieu, *Distinction*, 439.

2.2.3 The "Currency Model"

The problem is that alternative consumerism certainly did not evolve at the top of society. And, in this case, people do not orient themselves towards the top of a social hierarchy. Rather, they turn to groups and life-styles that originated at the margins and not at the top of society, thus certain groups of people, e.g. consumer activist groups or watchdog organizations, can potentially take on a guiding or even leading role. For a similar reason Grant McCracken introduces a model that helps to explain this condition; he calls it the "currency model." This model is essentially a modification of Simmel's trickle-down model, but with one crucial difference, namely that "[w]hat distinguishes the various parties is not their status but their currency."[63] McCracken primarily relates this model to the club-culture and explains: "[...] innovations occur at the margin of the social world and they move, when they move, towards the center."[64] Interestingly, a similar, or even the same, process of imitation and differentiation is still at work here. According to McCracken this happens in three waves: first are those who are closest to the "cutting edge of novelty," the innovators closely followed by the early second wave adopters who "give currency the new fashion." Consequently, "[...] the first wave abandons it, and the third wave prepares to adopt it."[65] At the same time, McCracken warns against thinking of this process as a youth culture phenomenon.

Despite the fundamental differences, the currency model does not preclude the use of Bourdieu's theory. Yet, in order to apply it, it has to be modified in a way in which status is not the sole determinant of the habitus, and thus of life-styles. Life-styles do not solely derive from the individual's position in society, but "currency" is at least equally important. This means that in the field of consumerism, due to the increasing importance of currency, traditional hierarchies may have dissolved, at least to a certain degree, which resulted in a less stable social order subject to quick changes. Hence, groups which are not at a high position in the status hierarchy, and which have their origins in sub-cultural or

---

63 McCracken, *Transformations*, 225.
64 Ibid.
65 Ibid., 226.

countercultural environment, may eventually evolve into a kind of social authority that provides consumers with decision-making input. In some cases, these authorities have become rather influential organizations and are now well established in mainstream society.

Against this background, it becomes less and less plausible that it is manipulation and the consumers' passivity that drives consumerism. Rather, it is the quest for ever-new innovations and trends, which, certainly, do not spring from a passive mass of human beings but from individuals who actively take part in the shaping of certain life-styles. This, however, does not preclude that other individuals may appear to be in some state of passivity – these would be McCracken's third wave adopters. Simmel, who already acknowledges this, differentiates between imitative and teleological individuals,[66] and therefore acknowledges the dichotomy of the passive versus the active consumer. Nevertheless, from today's point of view, he was unable to resolve the problem in a satisfactory manner. For, according to Simmel the teleological individuals would only constitute a small elite at the top of a social hierarchy, whereas the upward-bound aspirants would constitute the mass of passive imitators. The problem here is the same as with Bourdieu – though to a lesser extent – namely, that the theory is based on a certain upward-oriented dynamics. Thus, it is difficult to employ these approaches to political consumerism. As the term 'trickle-down' suggests, certain innovations or trends supposedly pass down the social hierarchy, whereas the general movement of the aspirants is bound upward. Whether this still applies to today's consumer society in America is highly doubtful. Their one-directionality restricts the applicability of these theories to modern consumer culture for the most part. Nevertheless, even though one might not be able to speak of 'trickle-down' effects anymore, this does not mean these approaches are entirely futile. Rather, some of the central ideas, especially the concept of distinction, are still applicable, though its causes and effects may work in more than merely one direction, and certainly not just up or down the social strata.

---

66 See: Simmel, "Fashion," 543; Storey, *Cultural Consumption and Everyday Life*, 40.

Taking up on the idea of distinction, Joseph Heath and Andrew Potter try to foil traditional consumer criticism by arguing that "[...] it's the non-conformists, not the conformists, who are driving consumer spending."[67] In order to locate the group of people they refer to as 'non-conformists', one needn't look to the mainstream, nor to the elites at the top of society, rather one must turn one's attention to the margins of society– to the rebels, who, according to the authors, keep the wheels of consumer capitalism turning. Thereby, contrary to many social critics, they clearly indicate that consumerism is by no means driven by a "quest for conformity"[68] – at least not anymore. Arguing that rebel consumerism, which includes consumer activism, is the driving force behind consumerism, they ascribe special importance to those groups which are generally omitted in traditional theories on consumerism. Nevertheless, Heath and Potter recall certain ideas of traditional consumerist theory and apply them to consumer activism, one of which is distinction, and by identifying the 'quest for distinction' as a characteristic trait of "rebel consumerism" they create an image that bears a strong resemblance to Simmel's concept of the 'teleological individual'. Consequently, it is not the 'elites' who are driving consumerism but the countercultural rebels, who act as innovators and trailblazers for new consumer trends.

The bottom line is that even though passivity might play a role in consumer behavior, and this must not be neglected, it has to be regarded as a sort of passive state that individuals can potentially elude. That is to say, this state should be regarded as to some extent controllable by the individual rather than an as enforced passivity derived from oppression and manipulation by the industry. Thus, it is not advertising nor the industry that is the primary driving force of consumption, but those individuals competing in the consumerist space while others may remain rather passive. Still, the notion of an entirely autonomous and self-determined actor remains problematic – especially in view of competitive consumption, for not every consumer competes for the same status or 'aspirational category', and much less to the same extent. Hence, the notion of a consumer who is not subject – at least not entirely – to the arbitrariness of the consumer

---

67 Heath and Potter, *Nation of Rebels*, 103.
68 Ibid., 104.

industry is an existential precondition for developing an understanding of political consumerism. All this seems to contradict Stuart Ewen, one of the foremost critics of American consumer society during the 1970s, who speaks of a consumerist world which "[...] consumes itself into social and political passivity."[69] However, the assumption that an effective form of consumer activism might exist means that one must abandon the notion of the passive and manipulated consumer. In this regard Jean Baudrillard argues that "[...] consumption is surely *not* that passive process of absorption and appropriation [...] [it] is an active form of relationship [...], a mode of systematic activity and global response which founds our entire cultural system."[70] Therefore the consumer must be regarded as an active agent who is, however, never entirely free from external influences and modes of domination.

2.3 Distinction, Cultural Capital, and Alternative Consumption

The striving for distinction is the striving for domination over the next man, though it be a very indirect domination and only felt or even dreamed.[71]
—Friedrich Nietzsche

It is doubtful that Nietzsche could have foreseen the dimension to which the pursuit of distinction would one day grow when he wrote these words. Then again he did name only one of the oldest and probably most characteristic traits of humankind. When the term 'distinction' is used in the context of consumerism, its meaning corresponds stunningly to the Nietzschean idea. The idea of competition reaches far back in history and has

---

69 Stuart Ewen, *Captains of Consciousness: Advertising and the Social Roots of the Consumer Culture*. (New York: Basic Books, 2001), 204.

70 Jean Baudrillard, *The System of Objects* (London; New York: Verso, 2005), 217. According to Baudrillard, consumption is "not only [a relationship] to objects, but also to society and the world."

71 Friedrich Nietzsche, *Daybreak: Thoughts on the Prejudices of Morality*, ed. Maudemarie Clark and Brian Leiter, trans. R. J. Hollingdale (Cambridge, UK: Cambridge University Press, 1997), 68.

come a long way – from ancient athletics, or medieval jousts, to modern day consumption. Competition can be centered on anything that requires special (physical) skills, and basically stands for the effort to become the best or most prestigious of one's kind. Nietzsche's 'striving for distinction' is at root nothing but a form of competition – the competition for dominance, and the same kind of competition that Bourdieu observes in consumption. In other words, even though the striving for distinction is obviously not a modern phenomenon, consumerism has proved to be a fertile ground for this. Heath and Potter even argue that "[…] the quest for distinction […] lies at the heart of consumerism."[72] They continue:

> But what we are all really after is not individuality, it is distinction, and distinction is achieved not by being different, but by being different in a way that makes us recognizable as members of an exclusive club.[73]

And, as with almost any other theory of consumerism, they put special emphasis on the idea of competition. At the first glance this may seem like an extension of Riesman's concept of a "[…] competitive […] drive for approval from the peers"[74] which indicates both the competitive nature of consumer society and the individual's sentiment of belonging to a specific group. But Heath and Potter's approach is nevertheless fundamentally different from Riesman's as they are based on entirely different societal ideas.

2.3.1 Keeping up with the Joneses, or Sticking out from the Crowd?

However, the idea of distinction which had already been emphasized by Veblen and Simmel around the turn of the 20th the century is fundamentally different from today's notion of distinction. It eventually became manifest in the metaphor 'keeping up with the Joneses' and was characteristic of consumer culture in America, especially during the postwar period. This was the time when the ideal of 'climbing up the social ladder' was the leitmotif for large parts of American middle class consumer society, which was determined by the rise of suburbia as the nucleus of middle class

---

72 Heath and Potter, *Nation of Rebels*, 213.
73 Ibid., 214.
74 Riesman, Glazer, and Denney, *The Lonely Crowd*, 82.

conformity.[75] However, with the rise of postmodernism[76] conditions changed, and contemporary theories thus tend to deal with distinction in terms of the individual's desire to stand out from the mass or rather than to conform. Underlying to this, according to Zygmunt Bauman is that "[...] postmodern society engages its members primarily in their capacity as consumers rather than producers."[77] He continues that along with this shift from a society of producers to a society of consumers came a massive decline of normative regulation, eventually resulting in the absence of norms. "No particular Joneses offer a reference point for one's own successful life; a society of consumers is one of universal comparison [...]."[78] Therefore, it is only a logical consequence that the essential implications of Bourdieu's concept of distinction go far beyond Riesman's idea of peer-group oriented behavior, which did not yet emphasize the striving for distinction as much as other theories on consumerism – Riesman's emphasis was more on a sentiment of belonging, along with the idea of social approval.

The group, which subsumes individuals who exhibit similar or the same distinctive properties that define them as members of that specific group, is a substantial element of the structure of social space. Thus it appears most appropriate to adopt a Bourdieuian position, for Bourdieu's idea of "habitus" is ideally suited to capture this phenomenon. Habitus being the "principle of division" is essential insofar as "[...] social identity is defined and asserted through difference."[79] Therefore, each group or class has its distinct forms of habitus, which may be regarded as the highest common denominator or intersection of all forms of habitus of each member. Habitus not only generates social practice but also structures taste, which "[...] is the generative formula of life-style."[80] And just as each class has a shared habitus, each class also has its distinct tastes. Thus, a 'life-style' as a system of practices, in Bourdieu's meaning of the term, is the manifestation

---

75 *The Lonely Crowd* has to be understood in this particular societal context, and therefore, it cannot so easily be linked to subsequent postmodern theories.
76 The postmodern shift will be discussed in detail in chapter three.
77 Zygmunt Bauman, *Liquid Modernity*, Repr. (Cambridge, UK: Polity Press, 2001), 76.
78 Ibid.
79 Bourdieu, *Distinction*, 167.
80 Ibid., 169.

of habitus and taste, as well as other distinctive properties. A life-style is thus the most obvious defining and distinctive feature of a class, or more generally a life-style group.[81] Therefore, a life-style group, according to Bourdieu's definition of the term, comes closest to what Heath and Potter probably mean by the term 'exclusive club' whose members' behavior is substantially structured by a specific kind of habitus.

Even though its adaptability to the United States might still be debated, the underlying idea of Pierre Bourdieu's concept of distinction[82] nevertheless seems to provide for the necessary tools to approach consumerism in America. Hence, some scholars have researched if and under what circumstances Bourdieu's theory could be applied to the United States. Here, the underlying question was whether 'cultural capital' could also serve as status resource in America. The key issue, according Lewis Friedland et al., is that unlike in France – the object of Bourdieu's research – "[...] the highest forms of culture in America are generally at best 'middlebrow.'"[83] Douglas Holt offers another modification of Bourdieu's theory by focusing on consumption practices instead of consumption objects.[84] The findings of both are rather clear; cultural capital indeed plays a role in structuring the social space in the United States. Hence, cultural capital manifests itself in "[...] the ability to distinguish objects according to their aesthetic value and thereby distinguish oneself from others [...]."[85] However, as

---

81   Here, to use the term 'class' seems to be rather inappropriate since Bourdieu's conceptualization of class refers to a different societal model. Besides, it is highly debatable whether the term 'class' in its traditional meaning is still apt to describe the American society. The term life-style group, however, allows for a more flexible approach, which is necessary for an inquiry on ethical and political consumerism.

82   See: Bourdieu, *Distinction*, 223.

83   Friedland et al., "Capital, Consumption, Communication, and Citizenship," 35.

84   The reason for this is that Bourdieu relies on examples like the fine arts as markers, or sources, of distinction among the French bourgeoisie, whereas in America the fine arts generally play a rather marginal role. See: Douglas B. Holt, "Does Cultural Capital Structure American Consumption?" *The Journal of Consumer Research* 25, no. 1 (1998): 6.

85   Friedland et al., "Capital, Consumption, Communication, and Citizenship," 35.

Holt finds out, consumption practices rather than consumption objects, which Bourdieu originally focused on, are among the prime sources of distinction in America. Given the marginal role of "elite goods" as a source of distinction, "[o]bjects no longer serve as accurate representations of consumer practices."[86] Thus, the focus has to be on the field of 'ordinary' everyday consumption.

Friedland et al. further examine the correlation between cultural capital and civic participation, which they add as a defining property to their appropriation of Bourdieu.[87] By including this particular property in their mapping of the social space in America they are able to identify a cluster of people who exhibit a rather high level of civic participation. The members of this group are generally quite well educated and at minimum attended college. Moreover they tend to have an average or slightly above-average income. Other distinctive characteristics of this group are predominantly high levels of involvement in community projects and environmentalism. The political attitudes span from liberal to moderately conservative.[88] This correlation of rather high volumes of (cultural) capital and high level of civic participation makes this group a matter of particular interest to political and ethical consumerism. The group of rebel consumers, which Heath and Potter's allude to, is to be found in exactly that part of American society in which a significant, if not the most significant, portion of political and ethical consumption supposedly takes place.

Processes of distinction are virtually omnipresent in American consumer society, and perhaps even more in the sphere of political and ethical consumerism. In this context, Clive Barnett et al. remark:

> One recurring concern of those promoting ethical consumption is the worry that this set of practices is the reserve of a relatively privileged stratum of the highly affluent consumers. This niche comprises those able to spend the time, energy, and money to buy organic, drink fair trade, and invest ethically.[89]

---

86   Holt, "Does Cultural Capital Structure American Consumption?" 5.

87   See: Friedland et al., "Capital, Consumption, Communication, and Citizenship," 39.

88   See: Ibid., 44ff.

89   Barnett, Cafaro, and Newholm, "Philosophy and Ethical Consumption," 22.

According to the authors this makes ethical consumption a mere "practice of social distinction,"[90] just as Bourdieu described. Also, this bears a strong resemblance to Heath and Potter's allusion to the pursuit of distinction as a means to become part of an "exclusive club." Consumer activist groups in particular may thus be regarded as just such a group. However, neither Bourdieu nor Holt or Friedland et al. take into account what role sub- or countercultural groups may play in the distinction game. Of course, one might argue that it is of lesser relevance when looking at consumer society in its entirety, but it becomes an inevitable criterion in the examination of alternative consumerism. Following Heath and Potter's argumentation, a logical consequence would be that the section of Friedland's model, which is populated by those individuals with a rather "high volume of capital-communal orientation,"[91] is exactly that group which matured from subcultural college-kid rebels into young professionals and thus made its way towards the mainstream. Being an acknowledged part of society then enables them to attain recognition from others.

In this respect, not only how, but also what, people consume is an essential matter. Despite the importance of setting the focus on consumption practices, one should also take into account that even in the United States distinction may also be marked by consumer goods themselves. Whether one prefers to call it differentiation or distinction, its central idea is also echoed in a variety of other theories. As Bauman puts it, for instance, the primary motivation of consumption is "being ahead of the style pack."[92] Heath and Potter apply a similar notion of distinction to their idea of "rebel consumerism,"[93] and thereby emphasize the fact that alternative consumption is essentially a part of consumer culture, and indeed, as such, consumer activism must be discussed in order to develop an understanding of political and ethical consumerism that can be related to the whole of consumer society.

---

90   Barnett, Cafaro, and Newholm, "Philosophy and Ethical Consumption," 22.
91   Friedland et al., "Capital, Consumption, Communication, and Citizenship," 42.
92   Bauman, *Consuming Life*, 83.
93   Heath and Potter, *Nation of Rebels*, 308.

2.3.2 On the Importance of Consumer Goods

Grant McCracken estimates consumer goods as "an important medium of our culture" for they provide consumers with meanings that may be used for the purpose of self-definition, and even counts them among the "most important templates for the self."[94] In addition to this, as Mike Feather-stone remarks, "[...] goods are used to demarcate social relationships,"[95] but it is important to note that, in some instances, it is not the goods themselves that confer distinction but their symbolic meaning. Thus, the striving for distinction may be regarded as closely related to the construction of identity – as an individual and as a member of a particular group. Of course, not every consumer good can serve as a means of distinction in equal measure, but those which do must feature certain qualities that make particular goods special in contrast to others. In his 1977 book *Social Limits to Growth*, Fred Hirsch calls these goods "positional goods," and his description thereof serves as an ideal basis for an explanation of distinction.

According to Hirsch, a positional good is generally characterized by its scarcity, a source of which can be either its limited "physical availability" or, even more importantly a certain "social limitation."[96] By arguing that social limitation may have its origins in a variety of psychological motives, such as "envy, emulation, or pride," Hirsch offers a toehold that allows for the interrelation of his theory with the various other concepts of distinction. Satisfaction is thus "[...] derived from relative position alone;"[97] that is to say an individual's position is only identifiable in relation to the positions of others. In other words, a distinct position is only discernible as such if the access to it is restricted, and others are excluded. It is only in this way that an object becomes a status symbol. Simply put, one person

---

94 McCracken, *Culture and Consumption II*, 3.

95 Mike Featherstone, *Consumer Culture and Postmodernism*. (Los Angeles: Sage Publications, 2007), 16.

96 See: Fred Hirsch, *Social Limits to Growth*. (London: Routledge & Kegan Paul, 1976), 19f. According to Hirsch, social limitation or scarcity means that "consumer demand is concentrated on particular goods and facilities that are limited in absolute supply not by physical but by social factors, including the satisfaction engendered by scarcity as such."

97 Ibid., 20.

has it and many want it. Hirsch also emphasizes the symbolic character of these goods which, according to him, is the "sole or main source of satisfaction,"[98] not a good's material qualities. The fact that these goods cannot simply be produced in large quantities makes them ideal markers of distinction. Thus, positional goods confer distinction in a way similar to that described by Bourdieu. Along these lines, positional goods would be exactly those goods or innovations that individuals seek in their striving for distinction. Because the prime token of positional goods is not their materiality but their very immaterial symbolic value, this matches perfectly with Bourdieu's ideas of taste, which, as a product of a distinct habitus, enables the individual to appreciate some goods and, at the same time, to depreciate others.

Bourdieu's conceptualization of taste, which "functions as a marker of class,"[99] can thus be perfectly adapted to Hirsch's idea of positional goods. Taste, as Mike Featherstone puts it, for instance, is an expression of "[...] the volume and composition of (economic and cultural) capital that groups possess."[100] Taste, in turn, manifests itself not solely in the interest in certain (cultural) goods, but also – and maybe even more evidently – in the specific life-styles typical of certain groups. This, however, is not necessarily restricted to groups with a high standing in the social hierarchy. Furthermore, as Heath and Potter remark, this also applies to countercultural groups that are certainly not atop a hierarchy but nevertheless actively involved in the pursuit of distinction. That is why the authors argue that certain life-style attributes like 'hip' and 'cool' may be considered as positional goods. As they explain, a central criterion of a positional good is that not everyone can have it; for instance, 'cool' equally constitutes a positional good simply because "not everyone can be cool." They argue further, "[...] being cool gets its value from comparison with others," therefore it bears a strong resemblance to social status, which is also a positional quality.[101] Bourdieu also highlights this idea of comparison with others in his statement that "[i]n matters of taste [...] all determination

---

98   Hirsch, *Social Limits to Growth*, 20.
99   Featherstone, *Consumer Culture and Postmodernism*, 85.
100   Ibid., 86.
101   Heath and Potter, *Nation of Rebels*, 191.

is negation; and tastes are perhaps first and foremost distastes [...] of the tastes of others."[102] Since taste is a marker of one's position in the social space, status can only be achieved and/or maintained by the disdain of the tastes – and thus the status – of others.

Although "cool is ultimately a form of distinction"[103] it contrasts strongly with the ideas of traditional status hierarchies – like those Bourdieu dealt with. Unlike the 'high cultural' forms of distinction, which are relatively stable, "[...] cool is structured by a restless quest for non-conformity,"[104] it is thus much more discontinuous. Nevertheless, Heath and Potter regard cool as some form of modern day status hierarchy. Likewise, Grant McCracken observes that "[s]ometime in the late 1970s or the early 1980s, popular culture rediscovered the status code."[105] Here, however, the central key word is 'popular culture', – the exact opposite of high culture – which is one of the central elements in Bourdieu's theory. Thus, even though status competition may have regained some of its momentum, status cannot be seen as a position in a social hierarchy in the traditional sense. Hence, the idea of status competition in Bourdieu's sense becomes especially problematic with regard to the conceptualization of the postmodern consumer. According to Mike Featherstone, postmodernism has brought along "[...] a process of cultural declassification which has undermined the basis of high culture - mass culture distinctions."[106] Consequently, the consumers' aspirations are not imperatively bound to one direction, and neither is the line of vision of 'status aspirants' upturned. As a source of this, Colin Campbell suggests that "[...] the fact that modern societies are characterized by multiple and diverse elite groups presents a problem concerning who exactly one is to emulate."[107] Thus it is fair to say that the days when few, or even single, unrivalled elites could dictate the modalities of status competition are long gone. By and large, keeping up with the Joneses has lost its importance in the competition for status.

---

102 Bourdieu, *Distinction*, 49.
103 Heath and Potter, *Nation of Rebels*, 191.
104 Ibid.
105 McCracken, *Transformations*, 201.
106 Featherstone, *Consumer Culture and Postmodernism*, 25.
107 Colin Campbell, "Romanticism and the Consumer Ethic: Intimations of a Weber-style Thesis," *Sociological Analysis* 44, no. 4 (Winter 1983): 284.

Instead, the society has become more segmented than into just hierarchical strata. One has to acknowledge the existence of different groups that are technically on the same status level – regarding income and education. Therefore, the strict demarcation between high-status groups and the aspirants may have become even more important since traditional forms of distinction apparently fail to fulfill this task.

For that reason, one must be cautious with the use of Bourdieu's concept – especially with regard to the question of whether and to what extent cultural capital may play a role in modern American consumerism, the setting of which, namely the contemporary American society, bears only little resemblance to the society described in *Distinction*. Of course, this is not to say that it is impossible to use Bourdieu; rather one has to appropriate a modified form of this theory that can be adapted to the rapidly changing values and tastes within the consumerist space, and which is less concerned with high culture than with popular culture, as Friedland et al. suggest. Hence, it is only in such a modified manner that one could use the concept of cultural capital to approach political and ethical consumerism. For only then can such immaterial attributes as 'cool' be seen as some kind of manifestation of cultural capital in the broadest sense. Consequently, this may also apply to political and ethical consumerism. One central aspect in the modification of cultural capital would then be to take into account access and the ability to properly interpret information on political and ethical issues, e.g. on sustainability, human rights and environmental aspects. This way the engagement in political consumerist life-styles could become a marker of distinction that would make for a distinct type of political and/or ethical consumer. The cultural capital in Bourdieu's signification of the term as the means and ability to acquire and to appreciate cultural goods like the fine arts then would only play a marginal role.

2.3.3 The Dynamics of Distinction and Alternative Consumption

Even though competitive consumerism is commonly regarded as the adversary of alternative consumerism, one will discover that nevertheless the same rules apply to both. As already suggested above, it is therefore helpful to regard political and ethical consumerism as part and parcel of consumerism at large. First and foremost, as Featherstone points out, "[...] differences must be socially recognized and legitimated: total otherness like total individuality is in danger of being unrecognizable."[108] Although Featherstone's approach focuses on consumer culture as a whole, and not on its political or ethical dimensions, this observation is most vital for the study of all peculiarities of consumerism including all forms of alternative consumerism. In particular, with regard to Campbell's findings, which implicate the existence of many different elites, the aspect of recognizability becomes especially important. For the elites, henceforth, must not only set themselves apart from their emulators, but must also establish distinctions between themselves and their potentially concurrent elites.

The recognizability, and thus legitimacy, of certain groups of consumers is an inevitable precondition for them to obtain and maintain a specific position in the social space. Hence, it is rather safe to assume that this is also a crucial prerequisite for political and ethical consumerism. The following example will help to clarify this: 'Rebel consumers' or more generally, consumer activist groups, which may be considered as some kind of elites or which regard themselves as such, do not just want to be seen and make their voices heard but also aim to make a lasting impact on consumer society. Therefore they depend, above all, on the recognition they receive from mainstream consumer society, which also means that a certain legitimacy of that particular group may be assumed. But considering the 'rebel consumers' in this field who are very likely to engage in various consumer activist groups, this also means that each elite also has to distinguish itself from others which are potentially operating in the same field and whose agendas might only differ slightly from one another. Consequently, it may be concluded that the consumer activist groups that are, at least to a certain extent, socially recognized and legitimated are the most effective. Otherwise, if any kind of alternative consumption and consumer activism were crowned with success, it would be most questionable, were it not for this reason.

But one will discover that there is also a central difference to the distinction process found in ordinary consumption: It is that political and ethical

---

108   Featherstone, *Consumer Culture and Postmodernism*, 85.

consumption is not exclusive by definition. Instead, consumer activist groups even try to advocate for their cause and gain adherents. They use a variety of different means to communicate their cause, such as magazines, the Internet, and public events or protests. Thereby, they manage to bridge the gap between the public and the private and put political and ethical consumerism at the intersection of both realms. The linchpin of political and ethical consumerism is information and its accessibility. The knowledge of how and what to consume, as well as the ability to put it in into practice, therefore becomes the main distinctive marker of a politicized consumer society. The information, through any channel, is quite useless so long as the consumer is unable to make sense of it. This is a matter of education and, to a certain extent, of resources, which seems to correspond to Bourdieu's concept of cultural capital. That is to say that not everyone is able to make sense of some kinds of information – no matter how readily available it appears to be – without the proper prior knowledge.

In any case, consumption implies the relevance of other human beings to the individual consumer's behavior. Bourdieu, Bauman, Featherstone, and Heath and Potter clearly stress the fact that any act of consumption is basically a form of social action. With regard to political and ethical consumerism, this aspect is all the more important considering the amount of communication involved. After all, consumers are social beings, and that means that one must conceive of the individual as a being in relation to the peer group – which is Riesman's principal finding. However, it is important to note that unlike Riesman's notion of a rather fixed and stable peer group, the contemporary notion is a rather volatile one. Mike Featherstone speaks of "temporary emotional communities" or "fluid 'postmodern tribes'."[109] Similarly, Zygmunt Bauman uses the term 'swarm' to describe what in his opinion has come to replace the group, namely "aggregates of self propelled units" with no leaders.[110] The temporal aspect, which both authors put special emphasis on, is an utterly important aspect with regard to consumer activism and alternative forms of consumption.

---

109 Featherstone, *Consumer Culture and Postmodernism*, 99.
110 Bauman, *Consuming Life*, 76f.

The ephemeral nature of consumption, which is emphasized in postmodern theories of consumption, is emblematic for modern consumer society, and thus political and ethical consumerism. This aspect of ephemerality becomes evident in a number of consumer movements over the last few decades. In fact, much of the cause-related consumer activism generally turns out to be a rather unstable phenomenon with regard to the number of participants. This is reminiscent of Bauman's idea of the 'swarm' as the prime form of social organization. For example, in the context of consumer activism, campaigns continue to gain supporters until either success or failure, then the numbers of participants may decline, who might then turn towards other issues. Yet, this is not to say that the decline in numbers of consumer activist groups is tantamount to a complete disappearance, just a smaller core group. This process is similar to that observed in ordinary consumption and in the quest for distinction, which oftentimes involves only a short-term involvement with certain consumerist objectives. Distinction is very discontinuous since it only lasts until it arrives at the mainstream, and thus cannot be upheld anymore. The result is a constant quest for new positional properties and markers of distinction.

The temporary nature of distinction comes to light especially in the postmodern context of consumption and consumerism. This temporality is not a recent phenomenon; all the theories and approaches, at least since Simmel, that deal with processes of distinction and differentiation have included this aspect. Bourdieu and, more recently, McCracken also acknowledge this temporality and both their theories ultimately pivot on this phenomenon. Bourdieu's model, which is based on status hierarchy, covers the process of distinction as a rather slow and protracted process, and thus has fundamental shortcomings regarding changes that happen more quickly. The currency model is designed to capture this aspect. Despite the fundamental differences between both approaches, McCracken's currency model does not prevent the use of the central aspects of Bourdieu's theory, it even allows for it. The reason for this is that McCracken's point of departure is also a status model, in this case Simmel's, which he modifies in order to analyze how distinction works in postmodern society. The essential commonality is how distinction works: according to both, distinction upholds only until it arrives at the mainstream and new forms of distinction have to be cultivated. By the time the 'masses' have adopted the markers of distinction, some are already preparing for the next thing to come.

Interestingly, the positions of the individual in the social space do not necessarily change after having adopted certain markers of distinction because this process does not initially determine where individuals are situated in the social fabric. Taking up on Bourdieu's concept of social structure, Firat and Venkatesh argue that "[...] structures may provide positions, but not necessarily the symbolic codes or meanings."[111] The former describes the position an individual occupies in the social structure; the habitus as mediating instance between the standing, and the social practices as well as schemes of perception and taste that generate life-styles.[112] The latter are not given; they are socially constructed just like Bourdieu's conceptualization of social practices, tastes, and thus life-styles. The volume of cultural capital determines the individual's capacity to decode these symbols and meanings. Even though the absolute position, which is determined by personal economic situation and level of education, is rather safe, the relative position manifested through the symbolic assertion of the differences, i.e. distinction, is constantly endangered by emulation and adaption.

Even though, only a comparatively small number of the aspiring adopters really manage to move to a new position in the social space, the groups, which are setting standards of consumption, nevertheless have to face the threat of becoming indistinguishable. That is, the mere appropriation of certain markers of distinction and styles by second and third wave adopters poses a big enough danger of a loss of recognizability as a distinct group. The consequence is then that this group he loses its legitimacy as predominant group. Hence, Bauman's argument that "[n]o lasting bonds emerge in the activity of consumption"[113] is due to the dynamics of the field, which result from this process of distinction. Don Slater vividly describes this process as "perpetual year zero of newness."[114] This is probably one of the greatest difficulties political and ethical consumerism has to

---

111   Firat and Venkatesh, "Liberatory Postmodernism and the Reenchantment of Consumption," 249.
112   See: Bourdieu, *Distinction*, 167.
113   Bauman, *Consuming Life*, 78.
114   Slater, *Consumer Culture and Modernity*, 10.

face, and this is also the reason why it inevitably follows the same rules as ordinary consumerism. Against this background, the quest for distinction in the field of political and ethical consumerism can, and must be seen as a means to ensure the group is seen, and perceived by others. Therefore, a group's legitimacy, once it is achieved, has to be constantly reasserted in order to justify their existence. Thus, akin to ordinary consumption, not just anyone can play the game of ethical and political consumption. As Steven Miles warns, consumption is "[...] potentially dangerous in so far as it accentuates social divisions"[115] and this is also true – maybe even more so – for political and ethical consumerism.

2.4 A Question of Choice

To conclude this chapter and to lay the foundation for the following chapters, it is necessary, at this point, to recall the question of choice. The concept of consumer choice is a central issue to all facets of consumerism; as Bauman writes: *"making a choice* is obligatory."[116] This means that, for any consumer, not to choose is simply not an option. This is especially relevant for postmodern consumer society, when "[...] consumer choice became the obligatory pattern for all social relations, the template for civic dynamism and freedom."[117] However, at the same time it must be noted that "[...] this exercise of choice is in principle, if never in fact, unconstrained."[118] This leads to the question of to what degree, if at all, choice can be free. It is beyond debate that choice has its limits that are socially and culturally determined, including social, political and/or economic factors; but within this delineated space choice is potentially free, though constantly under threat of being curtailed. The 'freedom of choice' is thus subject to constant negotiation. The liberalist notion of consumer sovereignty and the freedom of choice according to which "[...] consumers hold a very effective axe over the heads of producers"[119] simply because they decide with their spending power which producer, and corporation

---

115 Miles, *Consumerism*, 11.
116 Bauman, *Consuming Life*, 85.
117 Slater, *Consumer Culture and Modernity*, 10.
118 Ibid., 27.
119 Ibid., 35.

respectively, is to succeed and which to fail, is therefore more complex than it might appear. Even more inappropriate are the critical approaches to consumerism that tend to revolve around the idea of the consumer as subject to the dictate of the market. Since neither of these approaches seems to be able to provide for a convenient solution, it can be argued that choice can only be 'free' so long as it takes places within the boundaries of consumer society.

The boundaries that delimit the space of free choice are, however, anything but static. Rather, they are constantly changing so that a multitude of ever expanding and ever-new possibilities presents themselves to the consumer. And yet, these boundaries, and thus the possibilities of choice can be narrowed down substantially. Naomi Klein, one of the foremost critics of contemporary consumer culture and the corporate world, titles an entire section of her book *No Logo* "No Choice" in which she speaks of a corporate "assault on choice."[120] That is, large corporations press ahead with the decline of diversity by means of "mergers buyouts and corporate synergies."[121] As a result, only a few large corporations will be able to determine the range of 'genuine' consumer choices. And in fact, rather recent developments of the American "brandscape,"[122] to borrow Heath and Potter's term, seem to prove Klein's point. For example, the cover story of the July 2011 edition of *E – The Environmental Magazine* was entitled: "The Big Green Buyout." The article focused on the takeovers of formerly independent green U.S. brands by major multi-national corporations since around the turn of the millennium. Some of these brands used to be epitomes of green and, more generally, ethical consumption and consumerism. Ben and Jerry's was sold to Unilever, Burt's Bees was bought up by Clorox, and Odwalla – an organic fruit juice company – became a Coca-Cola brand,[123] just to mention a few examples. These can be seen as symptoms of a general trend of major corporations expanding their

120 Naomi Klein, *No Logo: Taking Aim at the Brand Bullies*. (New York: Picador, 2002), 130.
121 Ibid.
122 Heath and Potter, *Nation of Rebels*, 238.
123 Christine MacDonald, "The Big Green Buyout: Countless Green Brands Have Been Snapped Up By Big Corporations," *E - The Environmental Magazine*, August 2011.

activities into the field of alternative consumption. Furthermore, Klein focuses on what she calls "corporate censorship" as another major peculiarity of this assault on choice.[124] By depicting large chain stores and retail corporations, such as Wal-Mart or Kmart, as self-appointed guardians of middle-class values Klein demonstrates how their appropriation of these values constitutes a fundamental strike against diversity and thus options of choice. Thus, according to Klein's argument, corporations, not consumers, decide what is bought simply by reducing the number of options.

Indeed, there can be no doubt that, in terms of consumption, consumers can only choose from a preexisting set of goods and options available on the market. But these already existing options are not as restricted as Klein's argument seems to suggest. Instead, as Andrew Crane finds out, there is an "ethical niche market"[125] which aims at consumers with "[...] strong ethical preferences which drive their product selections and other consumer decisions such as where and how to shop."[126] The existence of such an ethical niche market, which was established in opposition to the mainstream market, suggests that ethical and political consumption can actually make a thorough impact on the market. But this is not to imply that the ethical niche cannot be corrupted by the mainstream. Rather, this ethical niche position has to assert itself over and over again in order to stand out against the mainstream. Therefore, it is most important to take into account how the consumer relates to the market by means of deliberate choice. Simply to state that there is no choice is not sufficient in an approach to alternative consumerism because acts of ethical and political consumption in particular require deliberate consumer decisions. Hence, one shouldn't just regard consumer choice as something that happens exclusively in private, as Slater suggests[127], one must also consider a political or collective-oriented dimension in consumer choice. As Schudson argues, consumer choice is maybe even the same as political choice in some instances.

---

124   See: Klein, *No Logo*, 165ff.
125   Andrew Crane, "Meeting the Ethical Gaze: Challenges for Orienting to the Ethical Market," in *The Ethical Consumer,* ed. Rob Harrison, Terry Newholm, and Deirdre Shaw (London: Sage, 2005), 222.
126   Ibid., 223.
127   See above: chapter 2.2.1, 17.

In any case, consumer choice can potentially be both – private and political – but it would be a mistake to reduce it to merely one of the two dimensions. This chapter has shown how consumption not only involves a purely individual dimension, but, as the Bourdieuian perspective suggests, also a considerable social dimension, which is reflected in the development of consumer tastes, which in turn conditions consumer choices. This aspect is especially relevant in the context of politically and ethically motivated purchase decisions. The following chapter starts with a historical approach to the relationship between consumption and politics in the United States, and then postmodernism, which is the cultural mode of the neoliberal order of society and the market – the arena for today's alternative consumerism.

3. Politicizing the Consumer in America

3.1 The Historic Roots of Political Consumerism

3.1.1 From the Revolution to the Rise of Fordism

Just as opinions on the political dimension of consumption diverge, for a long time experts have been at odds with each other over the emergence of consumer culture in America. Some date it back to the 1880s, to the aftermath of the American industrial revolution, and link it to the emergence of a managerial class.[1] However, more recently, the view that the foundations for the American consumer society were laid in the mid-eighteenth century, even before the American Revolution, has become dominant. According to James Axtell, the "English 'consumer revolution'",[2] which also effected colonial America, opened up an unprecedented variety of economic choices and consumer goods. Similarly, the historian T.H. Breen traces "the Birth of an Anglo-American 'consumer society'"[3] back to the same period preceding the American Revolution. By 1750, Great Britain had established a "virtual 'empire of goods'." However, this rapidly growing material culture also came with issues of economic and political dependency and imported goods were thus increasingly perceived of as "symbols of oppression."[4]

Most remarkable is that this rapidly growing consumer economy had developed without large-scale processes of production sustaining it. Breen also stresses that the pre-industrial character of the "Baubles of Britain," which the colonists wanted to shake off so badly, "[...] came not from

---

1   See: Jean-Christophe Agnew, "Coming up for Air: Consumer Culture in Historical Perspective," in *Consumer Society in American History : A Reader*, ed. Lawrence Glickman (Ithaca NY: Cornell University Press, 1999), 377.

2   James Axtell, "The First Consumer Revolution," in *Consumer Society in American History: A Reader*, ed. Lawrence Glickman (Ithaca, NY: Cornell University Press, 1999), 85.

3   T. H. Breen, "Baubles of Britain," *Past and Present* no. 119 (1988): 77.

4   T. H. Breen, *The Marketplace of Revolution: How Consumer Politics Shaped American Independence* (Oxford; New York: Oxford University Press, 2005), xv.

factories in any modern sense."[5] Instead, the early American consumer society rested on the shoulders of a sizable cottage industry back in Great Britain. The goods that were produced there had to be shipped to America bestowing in turn huge amounts of taxes on the motherland. Eventually the growing discontent among the colonists in this situation spawned the first boycott movement of its kind, which mobilized large parts of the colonial society to stand up against the British domination. The boycott of British goods was a sacrifice the colonists, men and women alike, were willing to take in order break free from the to the Empire's pinch grip. This decision not to purchase certain goods can most definitely be seen as a collective act spanning throughout the colonies. Breen sees this decision for deliberate non-consumption as an "[...] invitation to redefine private household decisions as public political acts [...]"[6] and – with this emphasis on collectivity – points out how consumption may even work as a motor of social change. Breen, almost casually, deems the idea of the self-sufficient Puritan way of life and the ideal of thrift and industriousness a myth, but, at the same time, delivers a powerful argument against the view of consumption as a matter of mere self-indulgence that precludes any kind of political action. After all, "[c]onsumer goods had made it possible for the colonists to imagine a nation [...]."[7]

As Breen vividly shows, a close connection between consumption and politics, or rather consumption and rebellion, have long played a part in American history – most prominently as the prologue to the American Revolution. Despite this example, it would be a mistake to conceive of it as a solid ground on which to base an approach to modern political consumption. Furthermore, even though Breen's findings may have their validity, the emergence of American consumer society in its modern form cannot necessarily be regarded as the product of a linear process starting with the Independence – much less can it be seen as a single causal chain. The marketable political attitudes of today are a far cry from political independence and the birth of a nation. History has taken many turns since then, and the mass culture of the twentieth century bears little resemblance to

---

5   Breen, *The Marketplace of Revolution*, 81.
6   Ibid., 25.
7   Ibid., 329.

colonial America. With the rise of consumerism, many issues not originally not connected to consumption have increasingly played a role.

In America, consumer groups, which can be labeled consumer activists according to the modern meaning of the term, were formed as early as the 1890s. The so-called consumer unions began targeting corporate monopolies. Tim Lang and Yiannis Gabriel give an insightful account of how something that started in New York with the establishment of a Consumers League in 1891 became a nationwide movement by 1898 with the National Consumers League.[8,9] Growing steadily, these early consumer organizations' main objective was "[...] the containment of the emergent powerful corporations." And, as Lang and Gabriel continue, "[...] these groups were concerned about the threat posed to consumers by increasing concentration and monopoly capital."[10] At the same time, however, the authors make it clear that the concerns about corporate domination over individuals as consumers also had very close ties to the individuals' capacity as workers. Yet, unlike its colonial predecessors, this kind of "[...] consumer organisations [sic] has no pretensions of offering a radically different vision for society."[11]

In fact, the National Consumer League (NCL) can be considered a groundbreaking force in terms of consumer activism. Arguing that political consumerism means more than just the boycott of certain products, Michelle Micheletti describes institutions like the NCL as leaders in what she calls "[...] *positive political consumerism* (so-called buycotts) [and] that encourage people to purchase goods following an established set of

---

8   See: Tim Lang and Yiannis Gabriel, "A Brief History of Consumer Activism," in *The Ethical Consumer*, ed. Rob Harrison, Terry Newholm, and Deirdre Shaw (London: Sage, 2005), 44.

9   Lang and Gabriel even identify an earlier consumer movement at the mid-nineteenth century. The "co-operative consumers," which they regard as the 'first wave' of consumer activism, and which "[...] began as a working class reaction to excessive prices and poor quality goods, food in particular." But since this movement emerged in England, which at this point in time already was by far more industrialized than the U.S., it appears implausible to adapt this to the American context. See: Ibid., 41

10   Lang and Gabriel, "A Brief History of Consumer Activism," 44.

11   Ibid., 45.

criteria."[12] The NCL's general secretary Florence Kelly initiated the White Label Campaign, which was launched in 1898 and lasted for some twenty years. This effort, which aimed at developing some sort of certification system for manufacturers according to which primarily female middle class consumers could make their decisions. The White Label scheme's call for transparency and fair labor conditions bears strong resemblances to contemporary labeling schemes.[13] Especially notable is the fact that the National Consumers League, which was founded by female social reformers and whose head was a woman, should become an important political platform for women even before the ratification of the Amendment XIX in 1920, which granted women the right to vote.[14] This is a prime example of political involvement through consumer choice.

However, clearly, this form of consumer activism, which Lang and Gabriel call "value-for-money consumerism," was entrenched in the cultural nexus of emergent Fordism and modernism. With the foundations having been laid in the late nineteenth century, after industrialization, the early twentieth century was marked by the rise of an unprecedented mass culture – mass production and mass consumption – as "[...] competitive capitalism gave way to the monopoly or Fordist stage."[15] The novelty that came with Fordism was what Antonio Gramsci calls the "rationalization of production and work."[16] He describes this as "[...] the biggest collective effort [...] to create [...] a new type of worker and of man,"[17] which not only initiated a radical transformation of the working environment, but also had a tremendous impact on the private lives of people. This system of mechanization, total control, and conformity would be the dominant paradigm in America for more than a half century. New technologies and techniques of production concentrated on the side of large, monopolistic corporations allowed for

12   Micheletti, *Political Virtue and Shopping*, 50.
13   See: Ibid., 50f.
14   U.S. Constitution amendment XIX.
15   David Gartman, "Postmodernism; or, the Cultural Logic of Post-Fordism?" *The Sociological Quarterly* 39, no. 1 (1998): 121.
16   Antonio Gramsci, "Americanism and Fordism," in *An Antonio Gramsci Reader: Selected Writings, 1916–1935*, ed. David Forgacs (New York: Schocken Books, 1988), 289.
17   Ibid., 290.

the fabrication of an immense number of standardized goods. However, in order to sell these products a market had to be created that could absorb the immense output that came from the system of Fordist mass production. Facing the flood of newly available consumer goods, the value-for-money movement saw its goals in "[...] enabling consumers to take best advantage of the market, rather than trying to undermine the market through co-operative action or political agitation and lobbying."[18]

To foster mass consumption in the early years of Fordist mass production, workers had to be turned into consumers. Firstly, this was made possible by increasing wages and leisure time that could be spent on consumption. Secondly, and even more importantly, the next milestone of this process of generating consumers was yet another "Consumer Revolution" to make the American dream come true – Lendol Calder calls it the "credit revolution."[19] The introduction of "an elaborate system of installment selling,"[20] as Lizabeth Cohen describes it, was commonly regarded among producers and retailers as an ideal method, which allowed especially the working-class to take part in large-scale consumption. Automobiles and a multitude of other consumer goods now being offered at large department stores such as Macy's became readily available to almost anyone – even to people who did not come from the old-money elites described by Veblen and Simmel only few years earlier. In fact, department stores played a vital role in the introduction of credit and installment selling, enabling those who otherwise would have been excluded from consumption to take part in it.[21] Thus, Fordist mass culture appeared to have a relatively egalitarian character, which seemed to blur class lines. However, the truth looked different; as Cohen contends "[...] mass culture did more to create an integrated working-class

---

18   Lang and Gabriel, "A Brief History of Consumer Activism," 44.
19   Lendol Calder, *Financing the American Dream: A Cultural History of Consumer Credit* (Princeton: Princeton University Press, 1999), 26.
20   Lizabeth Cohen, "Encountering Mass Culture at the Grassroots: The Experience of Chicago Workers in the 1920s," *American Quarterly* 41, no. 1 (1989): 8.
21   See: Grant McCracken, *Culture and Consumption: New Approaches to the Symbolic Character of Consumer Goods and Activities.* (Bloomington: Indiana University Press, 1990), 26.

culture than a classless American one."[22] Although Fordism might have been egalitarian in theory, it never was in practice for one simple reason: the money the newly 'generated' consumers were spending was not their own. And being debtors put consumers in an inferior position to those who do not have to draw on a credit in order to consume. Thus, if it were not for the credit revolution, Fordism would probably not have become the dominant economic and social paradigm in America.

3.1.2 Consumer Politics during the Depression and World War II

The Great Depression was the first serious challenge to Fordism, and was eventually turned around with the help of the Roosevelt administration's New Deal. The efforts made to stabilize the economy under president Franklin D. Roosevelt paved the way for the rise of the 'citizen consumer'. In other words, the New Deal policy makers began to recognize citizens as consumers. The way Cohen conceptualizes the "citizen consumer," which would dominate the Depression era, clearly involves a political dimension exceeding the vision of the competing concept of "purchaser consumers," whose contribution to society should be made through the mere exercise of purchasing power rather than the consumers' political assertion.[23] Newly created government institutions such as the National Recovery Administration or the Consumer Advisory Board were dedicated to consumer protection. Also, the Federal Trade Commission, which was founded in 1914 – well before the depression – when President Woodrow Wilson signed the Federal Trade Commission Act,[24] grew especially powerful during the Roosevelt era. Such federal consumer protection agencies provided a platform for consumers to get politically involved to a much greater extent than just being reduced to their capacity as mere purchasers.[25] During that time, Americans had become

---

22 Cohen, "Encountering Mass Culture at the Grassroots," 27.
23 See: Lizabeth Cohen, *A Consumer's Republic: The Politics of Mass Consumption in Postwar America* (New York: Vintage Books, 2003), 18f, 54, 56.
24 "Federal Trade Commission Resources for Reporters," accessed November 27, 2012, http://www.ftc.gov/opa/history/timeline.shtm.
25 See: Cohen, *A Consumer's Republic*, 18ff.

increasingly recognized as both, citizens and consumers. Eventually, as Cohen writes, "[...] invoking 'the consumer' would become an acceptable way of promoting the public good, of defending the economic rights and needs of ordinary citizens."[26] Therefore, the New Dealers paid much of their attention to the consumers who were considered *the* force that could restore the economy and eventually help overcome the crisis.

The efforts made by the New Dealers during "[...] the Great Depression spawned a larger reconceptualization of the role of the consumer among state policy makers and in civil society that World War II and the postwar period would extend."[27] This political reconceptualization of the role of the consumer went along with a stimulation of the economy by immense government spending. According to Lendol Calder, "[...] direct government lending became an important element in the nation's credit structure,"[28] and, in addition, FDR also took measures to stabilize the banking system.[29] Such measures were taken for one single purpose, which was to increase the Americans' the purchasing power – commonly regarded as "the key to recovery."[30] Simply put, as Claude S. Fischer writes, "[t]he Great Depression stopped the spending binge – but the Roosevelt administration tried to restart it."[31] In other words, the New Deal was an unprecedented large-scale state intervention in the market, resulting in a "triangular relationship [...] between consumers, the government, and business."[32] The effect of the government spending programs was not merely the reinvigoration of the Americans' ability to consume, which also allowed for the economy's recovery; even more important is the socio-political impact of the New Deal. Towards the end of the Depression decade, as Lizabeth Cohen remarks, "[...] the importance of the consumer in public policy and in civic life was indisputable."[33]

---

26   Cohen, *A Consumer's Republic*, 23.
27   Ibid., 24.
28   Calder, *Financing the American Dream*, 281.
29   See: Ibid., 283.
30   Cohen, *A Consumer's Republic*, 55.
31   Claude Fischer, *Made in America: A Social History of American Culture and Character* (Chicago; London: The University of Chicago Press, 2010), 68.
32   Cohen, *A Consumer's Republic*, 62.
33   Ibid., 56.

FDR's policy making clearly aimed at the enhancement of the common good with the consumer being its voice.

But, despite the impacts of the New Deal policy, the ultimate stimulus for economic recovery in the United States was World War II. Quite similar to the New Dealer's Keynesian view, stating that "[...] the government's role in promoting consumption, rather than directly stimulating investment was the key to economic health,"[34] large scale government investment in the war generated new jobs in a flourishing war industry. Even though during the first years of World War II the civilian industries and markets were subject to rather severe limitations and regulations, due to the priority placed on military needs,[35] the workers could eventually invest the money they earned in the purchase of goods, which then allowed for civilian industries and businesses to recuperate and even expand. As David Kennedy describes, by 1944 "[...] roughly half of the nation's productive energy was flowing to military uses" – the government's war spending was now about twenty-five times higher than four years earlier.[36] Finally, with the concomitant stabilization of the labor market, the New Deal's promise of a more egalitarian American society seemingly was about to come true. Not only did "civilian purchases of goods and services" increase by 12 percent between 1940 and 1944, "[t]he war even narrowed the gap between rural and urban living standards that had been widening for nearly half a century."[37] The fact that the Americans – unlike their allies – "[...] fought the war from an ever-expanding economic base,"[38] and managed to increase civilian consumption at the same time, was the vantage ground for affluence and prosperity in the American postwar society.

In terms of political dimensions of consumption, the war helped to accomplish what the New Deal had started. Especially the role of women as citizen consumers became increasingly important during the war. As Lizabeth Cohen remarks, "[t]he moral judgment of 'good citizen' took on

---

34 David M. Kennedy, *Freedom From Fear: The American People in Depression and War, 1929–1945* (New York: Oxford University Press, 1999), 354.
35 See: Cohen, *A Consumer's Republic*, 63.
36 See: Kennedy, *Freedom From Fear*, 645.
37 Ibid., 646.
38 Ibid.

new, gender-specific meaning in war time."[39] The definitions of loyal male and female citizens differed widely:

> Loyal male citizens were defined in productivist ways, serving their country by laboring in the military or [...] in defense industries. Loyal female citizens were defined in consumerist ways, as keepers of the homefront fires through their own disciplined, patriotic market behavior as well as through the enforcement of high moral standards in others.[40]

Even though women were increasingly entering the labor force, this conceptualization of women as consumers reflects, to a certain extent, the Victorian ideal of womanhood. In America, Victorian ideology had favored the role of women as guardians of morals and virtues and appointed them as rulers of the private realm, whereas men had to fulfill their role as breadwinners. Indeed, ideologues worked hard to reinforce this value system until well into the twentieth century.

The Victorian ideal of woman as caring wife and child-rearing mother emerged in the nineteenth century when family incomes, and thus living standards, had increased. In the increasingly urban society, a woman's contribution to the family income was no longer a necessity. The Victorian "[...] middle-class mother[41] managed the home, directed the family's social life, [...], and represented the family to the world."[42] The mother became the highest moral and social authority in a society that so drastically differed from its Puritan, rural antecedent. This shift from a rural to an urban society paralleled the often-mentioned shift from the society of producers to the one of consumers. With the rise of the mass culture and the consumer society of the early twentieth century, the Victorian ideal was repeatedly adapted to changing circumstances and even during the World War II period, its roots are clearly discernible. Now women "[...] were hailed

---

39 Cohen, *A Consumer's Republic*, 75.
40 Ibid.
41 Of course this is clearly an ideal of the middle class, which did not apply to working class women, who had entered the work force well before the twentieth century, because more often than not a working class family could not subsist on the husband's and father's wages. But, with regard to the egalitarian ideal of Fordist mass culture at the mid-twentieth century, this appears more than applicable – at least in theory.
42 Fischer, *Made in America*, 116f.

as the standard bearers of homefront [sic] consumerist citizenship, to an extent they had only hoped for during the 1930s"[43] – or ever. Nevertheless, the advance of women from the private realm into the public sphere as consumer citizens is reminiscent of the Victorian conception of a woman's role as bearer of morals virtues. Considering the socio-political importance ascribed to women as citizen consumers on the home front, one may argue that women still had to play some sort of motherly role as keepers of morals, and of a whole society, during a time of turmoil.

Policy-making during the New Deal and wartime encouraged political action on the part of the consumer. This political dimension of consumption grew especially prominent during the years of the Roosevelt administration. According Cohen, the citizen consumer can be seen as a product of "FDR's linkage of consumers to voters" and the efforts that were made to protect "[...] their rights as citizen consumer to fair treatment in mass consumer markets."[44] After the war productivity could be increasingly directed at ending scarcity in the consumer market. Fordism could reassert itself and culminate in the post-war mass culture, which was not only marked by mass production but also mass consumption. But new issues were about to emerge, since, as David Kennedy states, "[t]he War had shaken the American people loose and shaken them up, freed them from a decade of economic and social paralysis and flung them around their country into new regions and new ways of life."[45] This would be the initial condition of American mass culture during the 1950s.

3.2 From Post-World War II Era to the Rise of Postmodernism

3.2.1 Post-War Affluence and the Emerging Opposition to Materialism

The post-war years were marked by affluence, high mobility, and the rise of mass consumer society. But it was also an era in which many people became uprooted as old structures eroded and thus strenuous efforts were

---

43 Cohen, *A Consumer's Republic*, 75.
44 Ibid., 56.
45 Kennedy, *Freedom From Fear*, 857.

made to install a new value system that could counter these changes. With the New Deal and the War having fostered economic recovery and growth, the New Deal's promise of a more democratic and egalitarian America seemed to have finally come true. Millions of Americans could now enjoy the blessings of upward mobility as Fordist mass culture reached its zenith in the 1950s. It was the era of "High Fordism"[46] under the reign of a never before seen materialism. Having managed to overcome the Depression, and having defeated fascism, America could recover its self-confidence. "Economic growth and affluence, many contemporaries thought, were further eroding the class, ethnic, and religious divisions of American society."[47] However, this ideal of a classless American society would eventually turn out to be nothing more than a myth.[48] In fact, not everyone could equally partake in upward mobility; for the most part it remained reserved for WASP middle class Americans. Upward mobility also gave rise to suburbanization, which caused an outright boom in the real estate market as Americans moved to the suburbs in the millions and bought houses. To many, as Clifford E. Clark remarks, home ownership was the "[...] reaffirmation of the American dream of prosperity and security," however, at the same time, critics "[...] saw the movement to the suburbs as evidence of a frightening rise of conformity [...]."[49]

In many regards, American society was the Gramscian vision of Fordism as a system of total control come true. The fast-paced change that came with rising incomes and increasing social and spatial mobility, and which looked so promising, also had a downside as many were troubled by the quick and radical changes. Thus, all the more importance was given

---

46 See: Robert J. Antonio and Alessandro Bonnano, "A New Global Capitalism? From 'Americanism and Fordism' to 'Americanization-Globalization'," *American Studies* 41, no. 2/3 (Summer/Fall 2000): 38.

47 James T. Patterson, *Grand Expectations: Postwar America, 1945–1974* (New York: Oxford University Press, 1996), 320.

48 See: Jackson Lears, "A Matter of Taste: Corporate Cultural Hegemony in a Mass-Consumption Society," in *Recasting America: Culture and Politics in the Age of the Cold War*, ed. Lary May (Chicago: University of Chicago Press, 1989), 41.

49 Clifford E. Clark, Jr, "Ranch-House Suburbia: Ideals and Realities," in *Recasting America: Culture and Politics in the Age of the Cold War*, ed. Lary May (Chicago: University of Chicago Press, 1989), 171.

to the "postwar quest for national character,"[50] as Jackson Lears aptly describes it. America not only had to redefine itself; to a certain extent it needed to reinvent itself, especially in the face of the Cold War. Moreover, a redefinition of the system of values and morals seemed to be absolutely essential regarding the changes not just in global politics, but also in domestic politics. Almost all of American society seemed to be on the move, facing generational change, and also the abandonment of values like thrift and saving which dominated the Depression years. The effort to create a national character was accompanied by increasing conformity induced by mass consumerism. "Across the political spectrum, celebrants and doubters alike accepted the same basic assumption that postwar America was a homogeneous mass consumption society."[51] For some it was the preferable idea of social organization in the United States, while for others it was a nightmare, which found expression in the emerging critiques of conformity and mass culture during the 1950s.

With the onset of the Cold War, which was perceived as a serious threat to a society of prosperity and affluence, the United States needed to assert itself in order to prevail against Soviet Communism. America wanted to prove that it was the better nation – the bright land of opportunity fighting the evil, godless communist demon tooth and nail. Therefore, a return to traditional Christian virtues became a central element of American ideology during the early Cold War period. Yet, the value system, which was established during that time, had little to do with Puritan virtues of thrift and austerity. Rather it was an attempt to reconcile Christian values with the rampant consumer culture of tremendous spending and borrowing. And this undertaking would not be overly difficult in the battle against godless communism – distinguishing itself from the Soviet Union in this way, the United States could stand out as defender of freedom and opportunity. These ambitions for the cultural and 'spiritual' superiority of America in the world were a hallmark of the Eisenhower era, during which the phrase "One Nation Under God" was added to the Pledge of Allegiance. Even more significant was the imprinting of the words "In

---

50   Lears, "A Matter of Taste," 43.
51   Ibid., 47.

God We Trust" on American currency.[52] This was obviously an endeavor to equate American consumer culture with freedom and the virtues of Christianity, which were central to the quest for national character.

But the new value system also included a redefinition of the role of women, which, for the most part, seemed to be a reversion to the Victorian ideal of motherhood and domesticity. Against the background of the Cold War, when the whole of American society was seeking security, it was commonly believed that this security was to be found in domesticity. Consequently, women who had entered the labor market in comparatively large numbers during World War II, and thereby gained considerable independence in the public realm, were now increasingly pushed back to the private and domestic realm. The ideal of women as the stabilizing force in society not only bore strong resemblance to the Victorian image of women, it was also equally restrictive. This ideal of women propagated throughout the 1950s pervaded the labor market and even (college) education.[53] Women were being prepared not for career advancement, but for marriage. The whole system generated an image of women in which their single-most important duty was to become a housewife and mother – whose job it was to raise good Americans and to be "[...] a helpmate so that the man could rise in the world."[54]

Virtually the entire American consumer culture of the 1950s embraced this ideal of domesticity. The advertising industry and mass media, which became increasingly powerful institutions during that period, were also conducive to the propagation of the gender-specific role allocation of female homemakers and male breadwinners.[55] Even fashion reinforced this restrictive ideal of womanhood. Whereas during the war, when large numbers of women had entered the workforce, it had become "[...] acceptable for women to wear slacks,"[56] the post-war period fashion placed more emphasis on femininity. This may be regarded as a reconversion of the image of strong and independent women that had developed

---

52 See: Patterson, *Grand expectations*, 329.
53 See: Ibid., 367.
54 Ibid., 363.
55 See: Clark, Jr, "Ranch-House Suburbia," 173.
56 Patterson, *Grand expectations*, 362.

during the war. Even though being consumers was still pivotal to the role of women, the conceptualization of the consumer was much less politicized than it was only a decade earlier, when the state played an important role in the regulation of the market. As the state increasingly retreated from the market, consumers were recognized less as voice of public interest. During the era of postwar affluence the concept of the "citizen consumer" describing a person "[...] who consumed responsibly with the public interest in mind" gave way to the "purchaser consumer paradigm" that propagated consumption "[...] with the national interest in mind after the war emergency had ended."[57] This ideological regression separated consumption and politics in the public interest by making consumption a matter of national welfare in the cultural struggle of the Cold War. Consequently, the consumer movement, which had previously offered a political platform especially to women, became less and less influential.

The 1950s were also marked by generational change and the rise of a distinct youth culture. This decade also witnessed the emergence of the entirely new concept of the teenager.[58] Adolescence, as transitional stage between childhood and adulthood, practically did not exist before. During times of scarcity and hardship, as in the Great Depression, society had no place for such concepts. Instead, young people entered the adult world early in their lives and took jobs to support not just themselves but also their families. Only the affluence of the postwar period allowed for adolescence as a prolongation of childhood. The fact that teenagers now bore less responsibility than ever before, paired with an overall increase in leisure time, allowed for the rise of a never before seen youth culture, or rather subculture, equipped with considerable spending power.

This unprecedented generational change was perceived as a considerable blow to suburban middle class America. The youthful rebellion of the 1950s came up with distinct forms of fashion and music. Blue jeans, which during the Depression and the war had been only working class

---

57   Cohen, *A Consumer's Republic*, 101.
58   Patterson remarks that the term teenager "[...] came into widespread use only in 1956." See: Patterson, *Grand expectations*, 372.

attire,[59] and rock 'n' roll became symbols of the rebellious youth. Cultural icons like James Dean and Marlon Brando[60] were especially pivotal to the popularization of blue jeans, and youth fashion in general. An even greater shock was the rise of rock 'n' roll, when Elvis Presley became another hero of the new youth culture. Having its origins in African American music rock 'n' roll seemed to be a serious "challenge to the Hegemonic culture"[61] of white suburban America. Or as George Lipsitz states: "In that era, young people identified themselves as a self-conscious and rebellious social group [...] and their actions posed serious challenges to traditional cultural attitudes and values."[62] In the late 1950s the automobile, the epitome of affluence and prosperity, increasingly played a role in the subculture.[63] For instance a whole subculture was forming around the hot-rod and made cars into distinct symbols of the subculture. As H. F. Moorhouse remarks, the "[...] traditional 'work ethic' [was] now directed to unpaid time"[64] and spent on the modification of cars. This indicates how little the youth needed to worry about money and how the youthful rebellion was still anchored in the thriving consumer culture.

With rock 'n' roll and fashion blurring the lines of class and race, the youth had cultivated peculiar ways of consumption as statements of rebellion. In a way, one can speak of a 'subculturalization' of distinction, for

---

59   See: Sandra Curtis Comstock, "The Making of an American Icon: The Transformation of Blue Jeans During the Great Depression," in *Global Denim*, ed. Daniel Miller and Sophie Woodward (Oxford; New York: Berg, 2011), 23f.

60   See: Daniel Miller, *Consumption and its Consequences* (Cambridge, UK: Polity, 2012), 97.

61   Lears, "A Matter of Taste," 53.

62   George Lipsitz, "Land of a Thousand Dances: Youth, Minorities, and the Rise of Rock and Roll," in *Recasting America: Culture and Politics in the Age of the Cold War*, ed. Lary May (Chicago: University of Chicago Press, 1989), 267.

63   See: H. F. Moorhouse, "The 'Work' Ethic and 'Leisure' Activity: The Hot Rod in Post-War America," in *Consumer Society in American History: A Reader*, ed. Lawrence Glickman (Ithaca, NY: Cornell University Press, 1999), 282: "[...] by 1958 5.9 million teenagers had a license to drive and around half a million teenagers owned cars."

64   Ibid., 283.

only the young could appreciate the music, the fashion, and the cars – all of which may be regarded as specific markers of distinction for the youth culture. As an attempt to pull clear of the parental generation, the rebellion that accompanied this generational change was generally less political than cultural. Not just rock 'n' roll and the youth culture in general, but also an observable rise in juvenile delinquency, which was commonly linked to the rebellious youth, alarmed the moralists and induced a fear of the demoralization of American society.[65] Thus, all the more effort was made to reinforce the cultural ideals that were commonly believed would lead to America's cultural superiority in the world.

In the face of the Cold War, national interest was given priority over public interest. Consequently, the paradigm of the purchaser consumer became dominant, whereas the citizen consumer became marginalized. Furthermore, politics did not focus so much on the consumer as citizen as was the case during the New Deal and World War II – quite the contrary. One major consequence of the still dominant paradigm of "Fordist mass production," as David Gartman remarks, "[...] was to turn human subjects into abstract, calculable, uniform things, mere objects in a totally rationalized system controlled by and for others."[66] This was an ideal breeding ground for social criticism of all kinds with the Frankfurt School leading the way. Max Horkeimer and Theodor W. Adorno's *The Culture Industry: Enlightenment as Mass Deception* set the tone for much of the subsequent criticism. Even though it was published in 1944, a time hardly marked by a flourishing consumer society, it anticipated the outgrowths of postwar mass consumerism. They write: "Technical rationality today is the rationality of domination. It is the compulsive character of a society alienated from itself."[67] Indeed, the 1950s would be dominated by the reign of the expert – the American postwar society was marked by technocracy.[68] Nowhere else was this more evident than in consumer culture,

---

65   See: Patterson, *Grand expectations*, 344.

66   Gartman, "Postmodernism; or, the Cultural Logic of Post-Fordism?" 122.

67   Max Horkheimer and Theodor W. Adorno, *Dialectic of Enlightenment: Philosophical Fragments* (Stanford, CA: Stanford University Press, 2002), 95.

68   See: Theodore Roszak, *The Making of a Counter Culture: Reflections on the Technocratic Society and Its Youthful Opposition* (Berkeley: University of California Press, 1995), 21.

since "the central principle of advertising was 'science'."[69] And although Horkheimer and Adorno refer to the culture industry (i.e. the film and music industries), their criticism easily translates to the subsequent culture of consumption. Their argument that "[t]he whole world is passed through the filter of the culture industry"[70] is especially relevant with regard to film and later also television, which had been utilized as a means of communication by ideologists and moralists, as well as the advertising industry. Horkheimer und Adorno's statement is most remarkable insofar as television would become widespread only by the 1950s, when the culture industry would become the pivot of consumer culture.

Eventually the critique of Fordist mass culture resonated widely among intellectuals and was picked up by various other social critics and theorists. Most critics began to see consumerism as a mode of social control, which was geared towards the containment of the people by inducing conformity. Especially Herbert Marcuse, another major scholar of the Frankfurt School, would later refine this critical tradition in *One-Dimensional Man*. However, the criticism of the technocratic postwar society ruled by experts was not bound to Critical Theory alone. Among the most notable critics who were not part of the Frankfurt School was the American sociologist C. Wright Mills who admonished "[...] that the ideal of individuality has become moot" and that the human condition was to become "[...] what may be called The Cheerful Robot."[71] Mills' work refers to the increasing alienation of human beings and to extrinsic modes of control, which deprive individuals of not just of their freedom but also of their capability to reason. Furthermore, he anticipates some of the issues that would be central to Marcuse's *One-Dimensional Man*, which was published five years later and would become one of the most influential works of at least the following decade. Claiming that America had become a "society without opposition,"[72] and suggesting that "scientific rationality" had become instrumentalized and technology had thus become a "[...] form of social

---

69   Frank, *The Conquest of Cool*, 39.
70   Horkheimer and Adorno, *Dialectic of Enlightenment*, 99.
71   C. Wright Mills, *The Sociological Imagination* (New York: Oxford University Press, 1959), 171.
72   Marcuse, *One-Dimensional Man*, xxxix, 52.

control and domination,"[73] Marcuse would carry forward what Horkheimer and Adorno had begun.

Here one can clearly observe the common theme of criticism that took shape in the 1950s and which would remain the dominant form of not just intellectual criticism during that era. The postwar society of abundance was based on new forms control that had induced a quest for conformity among the majority of Americans. In other words, the technologized culture of mass consumption was bringing about a loss of individuality and the absence of reason. The result was a rather apolitical, robotic people in an automated society. Even the majority of the youthful rebels, who were challenging the values of the parental generation, but not the consumerist system itself, cannot be regarded as overly political. Nevertheless, the discontent with the rampant consumer society was growing not just among intellectuals. Small in numbers but widely recognized, the 'beats' centered around pivotal figures like Jack Kerouac and Allen Ginsberg were "[...] perhaps the most publicized form of dissent from mainstream culture between 1957 and 1960."[74] Demanding "[...] Americans must reject the excesses of materialism, conformity, and the consumer culture" the beat generation's rejection of prevailing social norms and conventions was "[...] a symbol of greater unrest to come."[75] Whereas the beats, who idealized anti-consumption, may have paved the path for the counterculture, it was the emergence of the youth culture that initially foreshadowed the end of the uniform culture of mass consumption. Especially the rock 'n' roll youth culture development of distinct patterns of consumption may be seen as an indicator of the imminent process of market segmentation. Both, however, were adumbrating the social fragmentation that was to take place in the following decades. Besides, what had been an almost exclusively intellectual movement in the immediate postwar period would evolve into a widespread social movement in the 1960s. Having his finger on the pulse, Marcuse's criticism would eventually be picked up by the New Left and the counterculture in the 1960s.

---

73 Marcuse, *One-Dimensional Man*, 160.
74 Patterson, *Grand expectations*, 409.
75 Ibid., 410.

3.2.2 The 1960s and the End of Mass Culture

Even though the success of Fordist capitalism in the post-World War II era persisted until the early 1960s, by the end of that decade the era of "High Fordism" was in decline. Overall, American society could still profit from economic growth and low unemployment rates. "Despite major growth of the service sector, manufacturing still drove the U.S. postwar expansion. Explosive growth of federally subsidized suburbs (single-family homes and highway systems) and of the standard middle class consumer package (e.g. autos and home appliances) forged a new mass consumer society." And in fact Fordism could once more gain momentum as "[i]nnovations and growth of mass media and mass entertainment, especially TV, and expansion of the retail sector revolutionized marketing."[76] But the 1960s were also marked by social and political change. By the late 1950s the Democrats were increasingly successful and formed majorities in the Senate and the House of Representatives.[77] Then, with the election of John F. Kennedy as president in 1960 the Democrats' success was cemented. Aside from Cold War issues the U.S. foreign policy had to deal with at that time, changes took also place in the interior. During the Kennedy era, consumers again were increasingly recognized as citizens, which had largely been neglected during the 1950s. Unlike hardly any president before him, Kennedy ascribed special importance to the consumer as the voice of public interest when he declared a Consumer Bill of Rights in 1962. This comprised "the right to safety, to be informed, to choose, and to be heard,"[78] and Kennedy also demanded it was the duty of the government to protect these rights. The citizen consumer finally triumphed over the purchaser consumer. This must be seen as a milestone in the history of political consumerism, for consumers were granted far-reaching rights in the market.

In a way, Kennedy's consumer policy had paved the way for the emerging consumer rights' advocacy of the 1960s. This new form of consumer activism often referred to as Naderism was named after its foremost spokesman Ralph Nader, who was also described as "the prototype of

---

76   Antonio and Bonnano, "A New Global Capitalism?" 36.
77   See: Patterson, *Grand expectations*, 441.
78   Cohen, *A Consumer's Republic*, 345.

the public interest advocate."[79] The large corporations that had become immensely powerful and whose growth had been practically unrestrained by state authorities during the era of "High Fordism" now increasingly ran into opposition among consumers. From that time on, no corporate activity could go by without consumers keeping a sharp eye on the processes in the corporate world. In the words of Lang and Gabriel, "[t]he consumer activist's role was and is to confront, to expose, to stand up for public rights, to be a citizen."[80] Consumer advocate Ralph Nader, who has been continuing his fight since then, started calling for corporate reforms from early on. Since Nader had begun with publicly targeting the American automobile industry for its inaction regarding effective car safety in the late 1950s,[81] a variety of issues had been added to his agenda. In a speech to the National Press Club in 1966 titled *Taming the Corporate Tiger* Nader criticized the corporate abuse of power and the insufficient, or even entirely lacking, official control thereof. Among the most crucial topics were environmental issues such as pollution and corporations' irresponsible handling of resources, as well as issues of health and product safety. And, above all, loomed the problem of "corporate dominance over local, state and federal agencies"[82] for which the consumer had to pay the price. Therefore, Nader regarded it as imperative "[...] to bring corporate powers, privileges and de facto immunities into greater conformance with the public interest."[83]

---

79 Richard C. Leone, "Public Interest Advocacy and the Regulatory Process," *The Annals of the American Academy of Political and Social Science* 400, no. 1 (1972): 52.

80 Lang and Gabriel, "A Brief History of Consumer Activism," 47.

81 See: Ralph Nader, "The Safe Car You Can't Buy [1959]," in *The Ralph Nader Reader*, ed. Ralph Nader and Barbara Ehrenreich (New York: Seven Stories, 2000), 267.

82 Ralph Nader, "Taming the Corporate Tiger [1966]," in *The Ralph Nader Reader*, ed. Ralph Nader and Barbara Ehrenreich (New York: Seven Stories, 2000), 136; See also: Patricia A. Sullivan and Steven R. Goldzwig, "Ralph Nader: Consumer Advocate, Lawyer, Presidential Candidate," in *American Voices: An Encyclopedia of Contemporary Orators*, ed. Bernard K. Duffy and Richard W. Leeman (Westport, CT: Greenwood Press, 2005), 332.

83 Nader, "Taming the Corporate Tiger [1966]," 136f.

Despite the fact that the efforts of consumer activism led to considerable successes,[84] it was not consumer advocacy that brought down Fordism. Rather it was the concurrence of various general political, economic and social trends. "By the late 1960s," as Antonio and Bonnano write, "race riots and campus disturbances, increased inflation, and socio-political fragmentation had begun to erode High Fordist consensus."[85] Society was increasingly polarized around various social, political and economic issues. The American society was facing issues of race and gender that had to be dealt with. As the Civil Rights Movement and feminism were on the rise, the demand for equality challenged the old value system, which eventually collapsed. Furthermore, the emergence of the New Left and the counterculture stirred up and radicalized the political landscape in the United States. Above all the social and political turmoil of that decade was the Vietnam War, which was incontrovertibly turning into a disaster and further fueled the growing social unrest. According to David Vogel, the emergence "of the contemporary political consumption movement" in the United States dates back to this time, and civil rights and the Vietnam War were among its central issues.[86] Social activists increasingly made use of market-based pressure to force corporate policy changes. Especially boycotts, as Michele Micheletti contends, "[...] were embedded in social movement activities in the past, [whereas today] efforts focusing directly on market actors are the main form of activity."[87] It is therefore important to distinguish between social and consumer movements because, as Robert Kozinets and Jay Handelman argue, "[...] consumer activists' ideological discourse necessarily views

---

84 See: Patterson, *Grand expectations*, 713: Patterson lists successes of consumer advocacy such as the ban of the artificial sweetener cyclamate and the pesticide DDT, both of which could cause severe health damage.
85 Antonio and Bonnano, "A New Global Capitalism?" 37.
86 David Vogel, "Tracing the American Roots of the Political Consumerism Movement," in *Politics, Products, and Markets: Exploring Political Consumerism Past and Present*, ed. Michele Micheletti, Andreas Follesdal, and Dietlind Stolle (New Brunswick, NJ: Transaction Publishers, 2009), 83.
87 Micheletti, *Political Virtue and Shopping*, 14.

consumers and consumption as the pivotal points for enacting a change in the social order."[88] Nonetheless, "[...] political consumerism is closely related to social movement activity."[89]

For instance, African Americans were among the first who used their purchasing power – amongst other pressuring techniques – in their quest for equality and social change using market-based pressure as leverage against businesses and corporations that would not abandon their segregationist policies. However, the idea of using consumption as means to political ends is hardly new, in fact African Americans made use of this power as early the 1930s when they launched the "Don't Buy Where You Can't Work" campaign.[90] And even before that women had pioneered political action through consumer choice in the early twentieth century.[91] What both the female activists of the 1900s and the African American activists of the 1930s had in common was that their agendas comprised issues that predominantly centered on their rights as workers and citizens, which oftentimes emerged out of local contexts. What was new in the 1960s was that consumption issues became increasingly detached from labor issues. Even though the Civil Rights and the feminist movements still put much of their focus on issues of equality as citizens, a general tendency towards activists' political agendas moving beyond just issues of labor and inequality was already observable. Especially with the emergence of the New Left, which "[...] was explicitly critical of business and the corporate system," consumer activism took on a new, larger dimension when "[...] during the 1960s and 1970s anti-corporate campaigns became a

---

88   Robert V. Kozinets and Jay M. Handelman, "Adversaries of Consumption: Consumer Movements, Activism, and Ideology," *Journal of Consumer Research* 31, no. 3 (December 2004): 694.

89   Lisa A. Neilson and Pamela Paxton, "Social Capital and Political Consumerism: A Multilevel Analysis," *Social Problems* 57, no. 1 (February 2010): 8.

90   See: Cheryl Greenberg, "Political Consumer Action: Some Cautionary Notes from African American History," in *Politics, Products, and Markets: Exploring Political Consumerism Past and Present*, ed. Michele Micheletti, Andreas Follesdal, and Dietlind Stolle (New Brunswick, NJ: Transaction Publishers, 2009), 64.

91   See the discussion of the National Consumers League and women's role in consumer politics above: chapter 3.1.1, 51f

major focus of the anti-war movement, as activists employed the techniques of political consumerism as a vehicle of anti-war activism."[92]

However, that period was also overshadowed by a severe socioeconomic decline as unemployment was rising and poverty spread. When President Lyndon B. Johnson declared his "War on Poverty" in the mid-1960s, the effects would bring only temporary relief. In order to "help people help themselves," the government decided in favor of tax cuts and financing education programs and job training, while federally funded welfare was drastically reduced.[93] However, the effects of these measures lasted only to that point in time in the late 1960s and early 70s when the labor market became crowded by millions of well-educated baby boomers and women who were increasingly striving for their own careers. Feminism had given rise to newly self-conscious and self-assertive women for whom having a job no longer meant an unfortunate necessity but personal fulfillment. Consequently, the rates of marriage declined as those who profited from the expansion of higher education entered the labor market. Young people, men, and women alike gave priority to their careers rather than to marriage and family[94] – it was the deathblow to the value system of the affluent 1950s.

By and large, the fate of Fordism, which had dominated the economic and the cultural landscape in America for more than half of a century, was sealed by the end of the 1960s. The fact that Fordism, which brought, in its wake, innovations like assembly line production, managerial hierarchy, technical control, and conformity, was capable of coping with the Great Depression and reorganizing the capitalist economy after World War II accounts for the great success of "High Fordism" during the postwar era. Yet the system was not prepared for the segmentation of the society and the market. The radical expansions of higher education and the service sector in the 1960s made for a situation Fordism was not designed for. Social change and the fact that, due to liberalist policy-making, direct interventions in the market on the part of the state and government welfare expenditures were

---

92 Vogel, "Tracing the American Roots of the Political Consumerism Movement," 90.
93 See: Patterson, *Grand expectations*, 535.
94 See: Fischer, *Made in America*, 137, 236.

reduced to a minimum forced the pace of the inevitable erosion of Fordism. In terms of political consumerism, the far-reaching social, economic and political changes of the 1960s marked a watershed, for it was only then that one could start to speak of an emerging political consumerism in the contemporary meaning of the term. In the following decade, the market increasingly became a platform for political action. The stage for direct political action had become neither elections nor the government but the market, not only for consumer activists, but also for feminists, environmental activists, and, to a certain extent, the Civil Rights Movement.

3.2.3 Consumption and Postmodernism

As the economy began to stagnate in the late 1960s and early 70s and unemployment was rising, the following decade could not meet the expectations of the people, some of whom had never seen anything but affluence. The various economic and political crises shaking up the 1970s would mark the definitive end of Fordism. The people's optimism began to fade in a time of "[...] collapsing faith in public intervention and planning, falling social wages, and ascending economic individualism."[95] The historian and social critic Christopher Lasch bluntly calls that period "an age of diminishing expectations."[96] An increasing number of Americans who grew up in affluent times in a society that highly valued the deferring of gratification and whose upbringing was closely tied to the belief in thrift as pathway to future rewards now had to face a future that seemed to be anything but auspicious. Consequently, this value system, which once was the backbone of social morale in America, lost much of its importance to many, especially young people. Instead, people now began to seek immediate gratification, which basically meant to live for the present and worry about the future later. Apart from this lack of hope in the future, another factor may be regarded as conducive to this emphasis on the present-day orientation. According to Colin Campbell, the widespread availability of credit had facilitated this hedonistic "spirit of modern consumerism," which in essence circumscribes the

---

95   Antonio and Bonnano, "A New Global Capitalism?" 40f.
96   Christopher Lasch, *The Culture of Narcissism: American Life in an Age of Diminishing Expectations* (New York: Norton, 1991), 53.

'buy-now-pay-later mentality.' However, Campbell clarifies that "[...] even with credit, the modern consumer's resources are still limited, whilst wants are not," which leaves the consumer in "a permanent desiring mode."[97]

Another outcome of this transformation was the redefinition of success, which Lasch argues was no longer measured by a person's actions and accomplishments "but their personal attributes," and, on top of that, "success [...] has to be ratified by publicity."[98] Or as Richard Sennett proclaims: "[...] what matters is not what you have done but how you feel about it."[99] In a way, individual performance rather than achievement had become *the* defining factor of success, which stands in stark contrast to the era of "High Fordism" during which virtues like industriousness and thrift were held in high esteem. Success and prestige were defined according to what someone had already accomplished in life at one specific point in time. The phrase 'from rags to riches' is emblematic of this ideal, for which American history can provide countless examples, such as the economic empire of the Rockefeller family. Thus, according to the Fordist definition, success stood for accomplishments of a useful life, far from pleasure and indulgence, which were to be rewarded at some later point in time. In other words, Fordism favored a society of millions of little Rockefellers. But far from a desire to conform, which is often ascribed to this ideal, it was "the apotheosis of individualism"[100] or the emergent "culture of personality"[101] which marked the advent of Post-Fordism and postmodernism. Paul Leinberger and Bruce Tucker describe this as the shift "[...] from the self-made man to the man-made self."[102]

Success and satisfaction cannot be found in the world of work, which may in part be regarded as the legacy of the Fordist regime having turned workers into consumers[103] and thereby separated the spheres of work and

---

97 Colin Campbell, *The Romantic Ethic and the Spirit of Modern Consumerism.* (York: Alcuin Academics, 2005), 94f.
98 Lasch, *The Culture of Narcissism*, 59f.
99 Richard Sennett, *The Fall of Public Man* (New York, NY: Norton, 1992), 263.
100 Lasch, *The Culture of Narcissism*, 66.
101 Sennett, *The Fall of Public Man*, 288.
102 Paul Leinberger and Bruce Tucker, *The New Individualists: The Generation After the Organization Man* (New York, NY: HarperCollins, 1991), 226.
103 See: Gartman, "Postmodernism; or, the Cultural Logic of Post-Fordism?" 122.

life. This may be seen as the initial condition for the emerging postmodern order. Due to this huge disparity between work and leisure, work had become a mere routine, a necessary means to an end, whereas satisfaction was to be found in leisure activities, more often than not involving acts of consumption. At that point, the consumer ethic had once and for all replaced the work ethic. The rise of bureaucracy since the end of World War II resulted in the growth of the white-collar sector and the shrinking of the blue-collar sector. But, as Richard Sennett argues, work had become no less a matter of routine.[104] Instead, workers have what he calls "a 'protean' work experience" which means that rather than on the appropriation of job specific and specialized skills, "[t]he emphasis [...] is on the 'innate' ability of the worker, as well as his interpersonal 'skills' of cooperation, empathy, and give-and-take as human being."[105] In other words, an individual is expected to perform almost any job on a given hierarchical level within a bureaucratic organization. Similar to what Sennett describes, Christopher Lasch characterizes the situation as "[...]the degradation of work [which] makes skill and competence increasingly irrelevant to material success and thus encourages the presentation of the self as a commodity," and consequently "[...] the only alternative to boredom and despair, [is] to view work with a self-critical detachment."[106]

This kind of detachment, according to Richard Sennett, creates a 'split self,' which means that "[o]utside of the substance of work an active 'I' is present; [whereas] within the substance of it a passive 'me' frames the self."[107] In this 'hostile' environment that bureaucratic capitalism had created for human beings, Lasch sees the reason for why narcissism has become "a metaphor of the human condition."[108] Or why, in Sennett's words, narcissism has become "[t]he psychic principle governing [...] adult culture."[109] This was preceded by a long process, the beginnings of which he traces back to nineteenth century Victorianism when the divide between

---

104 See: Sennett, *The Fall of Public Man*, 327.
105 Ibid., 329.
106 Lasch, *The Culture of Narcissism*, 94.
107 Sennett, *The Fall of Public Man*, 331.
108 Lasch, *The Culture of Narcissism*, 31.
109 Sennett, *The Fall of Public Man*, 315.

the public and the private began to erode. The prime reason why "public culture" has given way to what Sennett calls an "intimate society" is the irresolvable contradiction between "public behavior and personality."[110]

Now, as Sennett writes, "masks did become faces,"[111] which means that the emphasis shifted from public behavior, which Sennett regards as some kind of theatric acting or role playing, to what was beyond that mask, namely the personality and above all the emotions. This shift, then, gave rise to the "culture of personality" in which narcissism came to determine all social relations in such a way that people gain a sense of community through an "emotional bond" that "[...] consists of a collective personality which they build up through mutual revelation."[112] And this is the "intimate society" in which the emotions and feelings of its individuals are exposed rather than concealed behind a carefully crafted mask. Modern society was no longer to be regarded as a theater, rather, the actors have lapsed into silence and "[...] people have become actors without an art." But Sennett also highlights that "[s]ociety and social relations may continue to be abstractly imagined in dramatic terms, but men have ceased themselves to perform."[113] Thus, "[...] narcissism is the psychological rationale for the form of communication [being the] representation of emotion to others, rather than shaped presentation of emotion."[114] Although Sennett does not link his theory to consumerism, his approach is especially helpful with regard to postmodern forms of consumption, as the following will show.

From a postmodern perspective, Firat and Venkatesh argue "[t]he consumer should [...] be viewed as a producer, as well as a consumer, of symbols and meanings that are incorporated into the symbolic system that all human activity has become;" because "[...] production – of the body and/or the mind of the consumer, as well as her/his self-image – takes place in every act of consumption."[115] Similarly, Jean-Christophe Agnew argues

---

110   Sennett, *The Fall of Public Man*, 217.
111   Ibid., 216.
112   Ibid., 262.
113   Ibid., 314.
114   Ibid., 335.
115   Firat and Venkatesh, "Liberatory Postmodernism and the Reenchantment of Consumption," 258.

that "[c]onsumers invariably reread, reconfigure, and recontextutalize their purchases, and, in doing so, reproduce, recreate, and refashion themselves," he therefore regards consumption as "cultural work."[116] Hence, instead of adopting the modernist conceptualization of the consumer as a "cognitive agent," from a postmodern perspective the consumer should instead be viewed as a "communicative, symbolic being,"[117] as Firat and Venkatesh suggest. The postmodern consumer cannot be reduced to an actor (in the theatrical meaning of the term) who merely resorts to playing a role in a given reality in front of an approving or disapproving audience. Therefore the idea of narcissism may be connected to the concept of the postmodern consumer, whose behavior tends to be less of a ritualized, role-playing kind which follows an objective truth to speak in modernist terms. Instead, the consumer's behavior is primarily focused on the self, or rather an image of the self, rather than a reactive audience.

The image of the self, which is also central to the idea of narcissism, can be seen as a constituent of postmodern consumerism in which the consumer has become a symbolic subject.[118] Another important aspect of the idea of narcissism is that it involves both an outward and inward direction. On the one hand, there is an individual's personality and emotions that are revealed to others outside the self and which produce an image of a person, and which is, on the other hand, being reflected back at the individual – and this reflection is, so to speak, directed inward and thus may be regarded as highly self-reflective. Narcissism is therefore not about shaping the appearance or 'mask' concealing the self, but about shaping an image of the self – this image is thus an abstract 'representation' of the self, not a 'presentation' of one's actual appearance. And in fact, postmodern consumption has little to do with mere conspicuousness. The Veblenian "conspicuous consumption" of the late nineteenth century leisure class, whose primary concern is appearance and a good reputation, indeed has

---

116 Agnew, "Coming up for Air: Consumer Culture in Historical Perspective," 386.
117 Firat and Venkatesh, "Liberatory Postmodernism and the Reenchantment of Consumption," 258.
118 See: Ibid., 257 Table 2.

a certain theatrical quality.[119] Thus, from a Veblenian perspective, consumption is the presentation of one's social position rather than one's self or personality. However, with the advent of the postmodern consumer, people have come to act not just as an approving or disapproving audience of an individual's performance, but, in a way, have become a mirror for the individual.

From a historical perspective, it is rather debatable if and to what extent the idea of narcissism can still be applied today, but it nevertheless played a role in the emergence of the postmodern consumer. When Sennett's *The Fall of Public Man* was first published in 1974, the crisis had not yet reached its peak and the Fordist regime was just about to break down. Five years later, Lasch's *The Culture of Narcissism* was already written from an entirely different angle during a time in which America had to deal with a full-blown crisis. As economic growth came to a halt with the economic downturn of the early 1970s and the economy struggled with the subsequent recession, "[a]ttempts to solve this crisis gave rise to a post-Fordist economy, characterized by the flexible production of diversified goods on a new, global scale. This economy produced the new culture of postmodernism, which privileges difference, diversity, and ephemerality."[120] Consequently the market and thus the sphere of consumption also became fundamentally restructured. Postmodernism spawned a highly segmented market which consisted of "small, specialized niche markets"[121] and a society which had become more complex and more diverse than ever before as lines between classes, races, and genders had increasingly been blurred. As the segmentation of the market and the society advanced, the reorganization of the market into smaller niche markets opened up a wide variety of possibilities in the sphere of consumption. Yet, at the same time, the rise of "[...] *neoliberalism*, which stressed free markets and free trade and sharp reductions in the state's regulatory and welfare roles, was

---

119 See: Thorstein Veblen, *The Theory of the Leisure Class* (New York: Dover Publications, 1994), 52ff. The way in which Veblen describes consumption allows for the comparison of society with a theater, similar to how Sennett describes public culture in the 19th century. See: Sennett, *The Fall of Public Man*, 41.
120 Gartman, "Postmodernism; or, the Cultural Logic of Post-Fordism?" 121.
121 Ibid., 124.

hegemonic among U.S. policy elites [...],"[122] also facilitated a widening of inequality especially during the early 1980s.[123,124]

This age of increasing social and economic insecurity triggered certain anxieties among the people, since the social structure, which used to provide for a certain sense of security during the Fordist period, ceased to exist. Therefore, as Christopher Lasch argues, narcissism serves best as "tolerably accurate portrait of the liberated personality of our time" because it "[...] appears realistically to represent the best way of coping with the tensions and anxieties of modern life [...]." Lasch continues, "[a] society that fears it has no future is not likely to give much attention to the needs of the next generation [...] [and therefore people tend to] give priority to their own right to self-fulfillment."[125] Thus, in a way, the "ever-present sense of historical discontinuity" leaves the people with a powerful sense of the present. To some extent, this general condition leaves the consumer as a "fragmented" and "decentered subject"[126] with nothing to pivot on (e.g. the family) that might provide for some sense of security. Instead, Firat and Venkatesh hold that "[...] postmodernism begins to locate the consumer in emancipated spaces."[127] And, according to Douglas Holt, "[t]hese spaces allow people to continually rework their identities rather than let the market dictate identities for them."[128] In other words, rather than falling into a passive state of resignation or conformity, the consumer became an increasingly emancipated being. Therefore, people should not just be regarded as consumers of readymade systems of meanings and

---

122 Antonio and Bonnano, "A New Global Capitalism?" 41.

123 See: Gartman, "Postmodernism; or, the Cultural Logic of Post-Fordism?" 125.

124 With the rise of neoliberalism nothing had remained of the "triangular relationship" between the consumer, the state, and the economy, which was a product of the New Deal. However, neoliberalism did not dissolve this relationship, rather it was a consequence of a process which started in the postwar era. See above: chapter 3.1.1, 55.

125 Lasch, *The Culture of Narcissism*, 50.

126 Firat and Venkatesh, "Liberatory Postmodernism and the Reenchantment of Consumption," 255.

127 Ibid.

128 Douglas B. Holt, "Why Do Brands Cause Trouble? A Dialectical Theory of Consumer Culture and Branding," *The Journal of Consumer Research* 29, no. 1 (2002): 72.

symbols. Rather, as Firat and Venkatesh propose, apart from people's capacity as consumers, more emphasis has to be placed on their capacity as producers of "symbols and meanings," and thereby, the authors make an important move by redressing "the modern separation of production and consumption."[129]

Despite the people's anxieties, consumption has obtained a "liberatory" character not least because of the consumers' ability to produce meaning of their own. Postmodern consumption, according to Firat and Venatesh is "[...] paradoxically combining both the 'real' and the imaginary; in it, one can consume objects, symbols and images, increasingly recognized to be one and the same."[130] Hence, narcissism may be seen as standing at the beginning of the emancipatory process of the consumer that eventually became emancipated from (Fordist) orthodoxy and an overly dominant market. The ensuing focus on the self and individuality allowed the creation of spaces for new forms of consumption; instead of merely one single all-encompassing Fordist reality there was a multiplicity of possible realities to be constructed.[131] And the emancipated consumer became a central figure in this construction of reality. Thus, despite the profound social transformation, which brought forth narcissism, it did not leave a 'paralyzed' society of individuals who set all focus on the self and the present state of being. However, what has remained is the emphasis on the individual and the self.

Postmodern concepts, like Firat and Venkatesh's, generally tend to attribute a certain proactive behavior to the consumer. However, Jeff Murray and Julie Ozanne argue that "[f]rom a critical perspective humans are neither completely reactive nor completely proactive. Social actors are able to affect their social world, but this influence is mediated through the historical totality."[132] Similarly, Jean Baudrillard argues that, on the one hand, "consumption is a powerful element in social control," but, on the other hand,

---

129 Firat and Venkatesh, "Liberatory Postmodernism and the Reenchantment of Consumption," 258.
130 Ibid., 250.
131 For the postmodern conceptualization of reality see: Ibid., 257 Table 2.
132 Jeff B. Murray and Julie L. Ozanne, "The Critical Imagination: Emancipatory Interests in Consumer Research," *The Journal of Consumer Research* 18, no. 2 (1991): 133.

"consumption is *social labor*."[133] Thereby, Baudrillard also acknowledges the consumer as a "productive force"[134] though he does not necessarily see the consumer as a liberated being. This raises the question of if and to what degree the consumer can be free in his decisions (or choices) and actions. C. Wright Mills had already addressed the problem of freedom in the late 1950s, he writes:

> Freedom is not merely the chance to do as one pleases; neither is it merely the opportunity to choose between set alternatives. Freedom is, first of all, the chance to formulate the available choices, to argue over them – and then, the opportunity to choose. That is why freedom cannot exist without an enlarged role of human reason in human affairs. [...] the social task of reason is to formulate choices, to enlarge the scope of human decisions in the making of history. The future of human affairs is not [...] to be predicted. The future is what is to be decided – within the limits, to be sure, of historical possibility.[135]

This statement has not lost any of its significance to the present day. Yet, Mills – for whom society was a mass of "cheerful robots" – does not find an adequate answer to the subsequent question of who was to make these decisions. But the demise of Fordism and the emergence of the postmodern consumers provide an answer to this question. A consumer who is a producer of symbols and meanings, and thus contributes to the construction of reality, is therefore also a negotiator of choices that any possible reality may present. However, in any case, "[s]ocial actors [i.e. consumers] are influenced by constraining social structures; however, this influence is mediated by the actors' meanings and understandings."[136] Another important implication of the consumer being a 'cultural producer,'[137] to use Douglas Holt's term, is that the consumer being a producer of symbols and meanings can contribute to the construction of reality which may also include a future perspective.

This emancipatory process may also be seen as the initial condition for alternative consumerism to emerge. Considering the strong emphasis on the self, individuality, and the here and now, which Lasch depicted in his

---

133 Baudrillard, "Consumer Society," 53.
134 Ibid., 54.
135 Mills, *The Sociological Imagination*, 174.
136 Murray and Ozanne, "The Critical Imagination," 135.
137 See: Holt, "Why Do Brands Cause Trouble?" 72.

concept of narcissism, in addition to the low voting rates and the decline of political involvement, especially among the Baby Boomer generation,[138] the rapid growth of consumer activism may seem surprising at first. However, this is not as contradictory as it appears to be, rather, it may be seen as a shift in the representation of interests from conventional politics to direct action within the market. This trend may be regarded as a logical consequence of neoliberal policy-making. Since free markets with little to no government regulation were propagated, elected representatives of the people were rather unlikely to represent and enforce the consumers' interests in the market. Consumers accordingly resorted to alternative ways of exerting influence on the market. Thus, modern consumer activism, "[...] which emerged slowly in the 1970s and accelerated in the 1980s,"[139] may be regarded as a product of, or reaction to this liberalization of the market. As a result of the increasing environmental awareness in America, green consumerism became the prototype of modern consumer activism. Apart from the initial focus on environmental issues, ethical and political consumerism "[...] came to express concern over the panoply of late capitalist concerns ranging from human rights, unfair global trade, sustainability, corporate power, and other concerns of the global social justice ('anti-globalization') movement."[140]

The emergence of niche markets and the consumers' increasing niche orientation laid the foundations for this new wave of political consumerism to emerge. In the early 1990s, green consumerism was probably the first kind of alternative consumerism to occupy such a niche when it arrived at the mainstream.[141] However, the major difference to previous forms of consumer activism was that this new movement was not headed by consumer advocates, like Ralph Nader, acting on behalf of the consumers. Instead, the consumers themselves took action. This is partially due to the fact that the objectives had changed over time. Fighting for

---

138 See: Fischer, *Made in America*, 189.
139 Lang and Gabriel, "A Brief History of Consumer Activism," 48; see also: Josée Johnston, "The Citizen-Consumer Hybrid: Ideological Tensions and the Case of Whole Foods Market," *Theory and Society* 37, no. 3 (June 2008): 237.
140 Johnston, "The Citizen-Consumer Hybrid," 238.
141 See: Lang and Gabriel, "A Brief History of Consumer Activism," 50.

consumer rights and consumer protection, the focus of Naderism was on government policy, and one of its key successes was the installment of the Consumer Product Safety Commission, a government agency, in 1972.[142] Certainly, the newly emerging alternative consumerism movement could profit from the enhancement of consumer rights, but, in a neoliberal order, focusing on public policy would have been a long shot. Another central difference was that the new consumer movement actually "lacked any overall coherence."[143] Whereas during the 1960s one could speak of a more or less consistent movement, as consumer activism still had a collective character, the focus of the new alternative consumerism now was on 'politics' through individual, private acts of consumption rather than on government policy. Thus, close ties to everyday consumption, instead of abstract policymaking, was one of the main reasons why political and ethical consumerism could eventually become mainstream.

After the recession-plagued 1970s and 1980s, the 1990s under the Clinton presidency were again marked by economic growth and relatively descent prosperity. These years would also become the heyday of consumer activism and alternative consumption as the market became increasingly globalized, and as "[...] debureaucratized, decentered post-Fordist firms were ascendant."[144] Over the course of the post-Fordist/postmodern transition, "[...] the former 'counterculture' became the cutting-edge of the 'new economy.'"[145] The journalist David Brooks calls this new elite "bourgeois bohemians," or just "Bobos," and, according to Brooks, the "Bobos" constitute a new "educated elite." As a matter of fact, he considers them to be the "new establishment," which has taken the place of the old "Protestant Establishment" after the collapse of Fordism during the 1970s, and the associated social order.[146] Now, as it turned out, what Lasch had described in *The Culture of Narcissism* only a little over a decade earlier,

---

142 See: James T. Patterson, *Restless Giant: The United States from Watergate to Bush v. Gore* (New York: Oxford University Press, 2005), 116.

143 Lang and Gabriel, "A Brief History of Consumer Activism," 48.

144 Antonio and Bonnano, "A New Global Capitalism?" 42.

145 Ibid., 42; See also: Leinberger and Tucker, *The New Individualists*, 332ff, 341.

146 See: David Brooks, *Bobos in Paradise: The New Upper Class and How They Got There* (New York: Simon & Schuster, 2001), 11, 48.

would not endure. Even though the majority of Americans may have been disillusioned about their future, and self-interest had become one of the prime motivations for most forms of action, consumers soon adapted to these circumstances and became to a considerable extent – yet not entirely – 'liberated' from socially and culturally imposed meanings. The focus on the self and individuality would not preclude consumers from acting with a certain foresight regarding their future and that of the following generations. Rather, the segmentation of the market and society, despite the increasing inequality that came along with this change, opened up a wide range of possibilities and proved to be a fertile ground for new forms of consumption and consumer activism. However, this is not to say that previously existing forms of consumer activism have merely ceased to exist; rather one can assume that a certain "[...] convergence and cross-fertilization across the waves of activism"[147] has taken place.

3.3 Lifestyles and Consumption

As suggested in chapter two, traditional theories of class and status hierarchies are hardly useful for approaching the changes in society induced by the segmentation of the market. Although class lines increasingly became blurred, society was nonetheless segmented – yet not along strictly hierarchical lines. Consequently, a shift in theory was necessary; as Jean-Christophe Agnew puts it, "[...] the productionist, supply-side, and hegemonic interpretation of consumer culture has been shaken, if not overthrown, leaving one-dimensional man on a small and ever shrinking island of history."[148] Theories of consumer culture which tend to regard the consumer as subordinate to the market and the industry are insufficient for an examination of a consumer culture that put so much emphasis on the individual. Much less can such theories account for political and ethical consumption. However, this is not to deny the existence of an economic and cultural superstructure in which every action takes place. But instead of a predefined and rather fixed structure imposed by a small, technocratic elite, like in Fordism, this

---

147 Lang and Gabriel, "A Brief History of Consumer Activism," 51.
148 Agnew, "Coming up for Air: Consumer Culture in Historical Perspective," 377.

superstructure has to be regarded as something that is negotiable to a considerable extent. And the consumer being a 'cultural producer' contributes a great deal to the construction, or rather the continuous reconstruction, of this structure. It is therefore the consumer who has to be at the center of interest in a theory of ethical and political consumerism. Therefore, one has to take into consideration postmodern notions of proactive consumers without, however, neglecting the fact that consumers can very well be subject to manipulation and resort to a state of passivity.

Since class can no longer serve as an appropriate marker of social position, it is, at this point, necessary to recall the concept of lifestyle. This is important for two reasons: firstly the concept of lifestyles, as opposed to a rather fixed class structure, is more suitable for a postmodern society in which much emphasis is placed on individuality and/or personality, and 'emotions.' These properties are hardly measurable using quantitative methods like traditional categories such as income, gender age and education, which are used to divide society into classes. Secondly, a theory of lifestyle not only covers upward mobility but, even more importantly, it also allows for taking into account the possibility of lateral mobility. This means that a variety of lifestyles may exist among people who share the same "conditions of existence,"[149] to use Bourdieu's term. As Douglas Holt argues, "[c]onsumption is socially patterned because people who share similar social conditions acquire similar tastes that organize their consumer actions;"[150] therefore it is absolutely essential to consider categories that are traditionally used to define class. However, Holt avoids the term 'class' as he writes: "Lifestyles are symbolic expressions of collectivities that, through relational differences with other collectivities, map the cultural content of important social categories in a particular social context."[151] In doing so, Holt develops a somewhat 'postmodern' appropriation of Bourdieu's theory and thereby addresses Bourdieu's key shortcomings.

---

149 Bourdieu, *Distinction*, 166.
150 Douglas B. Holt, "Poststructuralist Lifestyle Analysis: Conceptualizing the Social Patterning of Consumption in Postmodernity," *The Journal of Consumer Research* 23, no. 4 (1997): 343.
151 Ibid.

What Holt primarily objects to regarding Bourdieu's lifestyle concept is that, for Bourdieu, lifestyles are the site for social reproduction, rather than for social production. Accordingly, consuming is "[…] a social activity in which consumption objects are used as resources to interact with others," It would then be nothing but the enactment of tastes "[…] through particular consumption practices, [and thereby people enact] symbolic boundaries that affirm distinctions between collectivities." Thus, lifestyles, through which collectivity is expressed by means of the "enactment of tastes in everyday life," serve to "reproduce social relations."[152] However, Holt does not falsify the Bourdieuian perspective, rather he contends that "[…] the expression of collectivity through lifestyle serves to either reproduce or transform the collectivity."[153] Compared to Bourdieu, this particular notion of lifestyle, which includes the idea of social transformation and thus also comprises the possibility of social and cultural production – in addition to the idea of social reproduction – makes it a more flexible and useful approach, especially in conjunction with postmodern conceptualizations of the consumer and consumer agency.

Even though there is every indication that social hierarchies have not ceased to exist with the erosion of Fordism, it is fair to assume that these hierarchies have become more permeable. As David Brooks suggests, the new Bobo elite culture is essentially a meritocracy in which mobility essentially depends on individual ability and not on ancestry or wealth.[154] In other words, individual achievement and success, rather than simply being born into a high status group, may be regarded as a powerful source of social status and prestige in the contemporary American society. And this change made its presence felt in the social world, as well as in the world of employment. Similarly, Antonio and Bonnano illustrate how the outcome of Fordism's breakdown was a "[…] fundamentally restructured

---

152 Holt, "Poststructuralist Lifestyle Analysis," 343.
153 Ibid., 344. Nevertheless, Holt also considers the fact that "lifestyles can also serve as potent exclusionary devices, limiting the social mobility of less endowed groups." Despite the transformational potential he ascribes to lifestyles, Holt also acknowledges the fact that the "privileged tastes" which are "naturalized in elite groups" include the depreciation of the tastes of the less privileged, which corresponds to Bourdieu's conceptualization of taste.
154 See: Brooks, *Bobos in Paradise*, 27ff.

U.S. capitalism that was characterized by technically transformed workplaces, organizations, and neighborhoods; was linked by knowledge-based 'networks'; and that afforded able individuals nearly infinite opportunities for advancement or lateral movement."[155] And it is exactly this lateral movement, especially with regard to social mobility, which is an important aspect with regard to lifestyles.

For Bourdieu, lifestyles serve as the basis for social reproduction of a distinct class: each class exhibits certain distinctive features that delineate the differences to other classes, and thereby lifestyles serve to maintain the social hierarchy.[156] In other words, Bourdieu assumes a strictly vertically organized society. But as Holt rightly suggests, lifestyles may also serve to transform this hierarchy. Furthermore, the central implication of the idea of lateral movement is that there is not just one single elite, with one particular value system – like the WASP elite during the Fordist period. Rather, there may be a variety of coexisting lifestyles on the same hierarchical level. And even though the "Bobos" may be the new and dominant elite, this does not mean that there are no other elitist groups, which have cultivated their particular elitist lifestyles. For instance the WASPs, though they may have lost their status as single most dominant elite, may still be considered a force to reckon with. Therefore, in a society in which lifestyles may potentially coexist, individuals can move "[...] from the margins to the center of society. In this case, they are moving not upward in social space but across it."[157] Hence, the struggle is not between classes, as the Marxist rhetoric suggests, but rather between different lifestyle groups, wherein currency rather than status is the primary goal of the striving for distinction. And, following McCracken, this may be considered as true for elites as it is for subcultures or youth cultures.[158]

Speaking of lifestyles, which are cultivated by members of specific social groups, means speaking of a group whose members generally share a common set of values, which may include specific forms of knowledge and a similar, if not identical, political attitudes. Apart from that, the members of a lifestyle group share the same ways and means of communication.

---

155 Antonio and Bonnano, "A New Global Capitalism?" 41f.
156 See: Bourdieu, *Distinction*, 255.
157 McCracken, *Transformations*, 71.
158 McCracken's "currency model" was discussed earlier in chapter 2.2.3, 27.

All of which is reflected in the way consumer choices are made, which then more often than not results in some sort of shared fashion, that may serve as a means to set oneself apart from individuals belonging to a different lifestyle group. In other words, not only the goods being purchased but also the way in which decisions are made convey distinction of a certain kind. One will find that distinction is still at work; only it is not exclusively the realm of a small elite to which the less privileged aspire. Rather different lifestyles develop different forms of distinction. Therefore, distinction cannot be regarded as a demarcation between an elite and a lower group of people. Rather distinction works in many directions, in addition to the earlier notions of distinction, like those of Veblen, Simmel or Bourdieu, which all, to a certain extent, include some form of trickle down effect. Aside from this kind of 'vertical' distinction, one has to take into consideration the possibility of 'lateral' distinction, which may be at work between different collectivities on the same social level. Furthermore, vertical distinction works not just in a downward direction, but may also work in an upward direction.

This sense distinction from above may be found in subcultures, and especially in the counterculture of the 1960s in which a profound anti-establishment sentiment was prevalent. Now, the Bobos who grew out of this countercultural context, and who now constitute the "educated elite," are, according to Brooks, "[...] repelled by the idea of keeping up with the Joneses."[159] Members of this particular lifestyle group generally despise rampant and conspicuous consumption, rather they clearly fit into the pattern of postmodern consumers and consumption, which Mike Featherstone describes as follows:

> Rather than unreflexively adopting a lifestyle, through tradition or habit, the new heroes of consumer culture make lifestyle a life project and display their individuality and sense of style in the particularity of the assemblage of goods, clothes, practices, experiences, appearance and bodily dispositions they design together into a lifestyle. The modern individual [...] speaks not only with his clothes, but with his home, furnishings, interior decoration, car and other activities which are to be read and classified in terms of the presence and absence of taste.[160]

---

159 Brooks, *Bobos in Paradise*, 93.
160 Featherstone, *Consumer Culture and Postmodernism*, 84.

Thus, with the rise of Post-Fordism and postmodernism, the fragmentation of the consumer and society, as well as the segmentation of the market, the use of emulative models of society, which might have offered apt descriptions of a Fordist consumer society like those of Veblen and Simmel, has for the most part become obsolete. Even Bourdieu cannot be entirely adapted to this radically altered society – at least not without major modifications. Therefore, one has to rely on other theories or concepts, like McCracken's currency model, which allows for a more precise examination of a highly segmented society without neglecting the hierarchical structures of society.

Consumption has become a substantial, yet not independent, "dimension of social life." As Holt remarks, "[...] although other dimensions of social life such as the political, economic, technical, and religious spheres are distinct from consumption, they are not autonomous and, so, often interact with consumption patterns."[161] This is important in so far, as consumption is not merely regarded as "an auxiliary to work,"[162] as in Fordism and its contemporary theories. Rather, the fact that these different spheres may interact creates the prerequisites for contemporary forms of alternative consumption and consumer activism. And in a way this corresponds to the postmodern notion of consumption as a form of cultural production. Even though one may argue that there have always been certain political and ethical dimensions to consumption, it was only in the late twentieth century, after the 'cheerful robots' became animate, that one could begin to speak of ethical and political consumerism, as we know it today. This chapter has put the relationship between politics and consumption in a historical perspective, and this is important for understanding the political dimensions of modern consumption – especially since the breakdown of Fordism. The following chapter elaborates on how alternative consumption and contemporary consumer activism operate within the market.

---

161   Holt, "Poststructuralist Lifestyle Analysis," 343f.
162   Featherstone, *Consumer Culture and Postmodernism*, 21.

4. Mobilizing Consumers

4.1 Alternative Consumption in the Age of the Superbrand

Decisions like whether to choose a paper bag or plastic one at the register in the supermarket or a Toyota Prius over a gas-guzzling SUV are two of the simplest ethical choices to be made in ordinary consumption decisions. In fact, considerable portions of ethical and political consumption take place within the scope of everyday consumption. But alternative consumerism and consumer activism is more extensive than that by far. It ranges from reform to subversion, and Robert Kozinets and Jay Handelman even speak of a radicalization of consumption.[1]

After the Cold War ended, neoliberalism and globalization gave rise to an era which Naomi Klein labels "The Age of the Superbrand." These Superbrands are by definition large, multinational corporations whose core business is not manufacturing, but "brand building." As these corporations have outsourced their production, brand builders have become "the new primary producers."[2] In other words, these companies sell, but they do not produce. And this development has made its impact on the social organization, because, in the postmodern definition of consumerism, considerable parts of society and social relations are organized around consumption. Even more specifically, Albert Muniz and Thomas O'Guinn argue that not only most social interaction, but also the entire society pivots around brands. Hence they develop their concept of "brand community," which describes communities that center on "a branded good or service." And this new form of "imagined community,"[3] brand loyalty, serves as a

---

1   See: Kozinets and Handelman, "Adversaries of Consumption," 692.
2   Klein, *No Logo*, 196.
3   Albert M. Muniz and Thomas C. O'Guinn, "Brand Community," *The Journal of Consumer Research* 27, no. 4 (2001): 419. They also write: "Brand communities are largely imagined communities. Members feel part of a large, unmet, but easily imagined community." Thereby they draw on Benedict Anderson's concept of "imagined communities" which is intrinsically a theory of nationalism, and not of consumerism; See also: Benedict Anderson, *Imagined Communities: Reflections on the Origin and Spread of Nationalism* (London; New York: Verso, 1991), 6. Anderson writes that a national community "[...] is *imagined* because the members of even the smallest nation will never

means of social cohesion. However, they also contend that a brand community cannot be regarded as a "homogenous lifestyle segment," mainly because they are less stable and their membership is much less consistent than it is usually assumed to be in the case of lifestyle groups.[4] Similarly, Douglas Holt even devises a "post-postmodern condition" in which "[...] brands will become another form of expressive culture" whereby individuals develop "brand assisted identities." As a consequence, Holt predicts "[t]he proliferation of narrowly focused consumption communities."[5] However, this does not mean one has to abandon lifestyle theory. Instead, one may regard Muniz and O'Guinn's idea of brand community as supplementary to lifestyles insofar as brands may serve as a means of cultural production. With regard to ethical and political consumerism, brands may also serve as a resource for collective and individual identities. However, this does not work in the same way as in brand or consumption communities; with brands as "corporate adversaries,"[6] they may fulfil a central role in identity formation by means of negative definition. Since much of contemporary activism works this way, this shows how deeply consumer activism is intertwined with the consumerist nexus.[7]

Due to the omnipresence of brands in consumer society in which, Klein claims, "[...] malls have become the modern town square,"[8] everything from simple messages to social relations become mediated through the market[9] as the consumer is flooded by branded messages of various kinds, and many community matters revolve around consumption. However,

---

know most of their fellow-members, meet them, or even hear of them, yet in the minds of each lives the image of their communion." And as Muniz and O'Guinn find this also applies to a considerable extent to consumption communities and the sense of identification of its members.

4   See: Muniz and O'Guinn, "Brand Community," 412, 426.
5   Holt, "Why Do Brands Cause Trouble?" 87.
6   Kozinets and Handelman, "Adversaries of Consumption," 697.
7   Even Richard Sennett's theory, despite its critical tone, already acknowledges a similar correlation between rebellion and capitalism. For him, it is capitalism, which - though indirectly - produces personality as people "revolt against its evils." See: Sennett, *The Fall of Public Man*, 295.
8   Klein, *No Logo*, 183.
9   This image is evocative of Horkheimer und Adorno's description of the "culture industry" through which everything is "filtered." See above: chapter 3.2.1, 65.

branding is only the tip of the iceberg for it was the business practices of the multinational "superbrand" corporations which initially spurred consumer resistance during the 1990s and which gave new impulse to consumer activism and alternative consumption in general. As the call for corporate social responsibility became louder, ways of protesting became more radical. Anti-corporate activism gained momentum and green consumerism could reassert itself, and, in the wake of the polarization of the consumer market, ethical niche markets such as fair trade and organic food markets began to flourish and still do. But whereas these forms still involve consumption, other movements promoting lifestyles which involve the reduction of consumption, or even anti-consumption, have been increasingly in vogue ever since. So-called freecycle communities and the Voluntary Simplicity Movement[10] actively promote a reduction of consumption in order to enhance the quality of living. Culture Jamming, which can also be labeled anti-consumerist, is another movement primarily consisting of anti-brand activists aiming at advertising messages and brand images, and will be discussed in detail below.

While the aforementioned movements aim at the subversion of the consumerist system as it is, traditional forms of consumer activism that act within the boundaries of the market, i.e. consumer advocacy, still exist and must be seen as an integral part of the consumerist landscape. Non-governmental organizations like Public Citizen epitomize the legacy of Naderism. Founded by Ralph Nader in 1971,[11] this organization has become an influential institution lobbying consumers and the public interest and forcing the government to act in the interest of the people. For example, one of the successes for which Public Citizen claims credit is the foundation of the Consumer Financial Protection Bureau within the context of the *Dodd-Frank Wall Street Reform and Consumer Protection*

---

10 See: Nelson, Rademacher, and Paek, "Downshifting Consumer = Upshifting Citizen?" 151; Samuel Alexander and Simon Ussher, "The Voluntary Simplicity Movement: A Multi-national Survey Analysis in Theoretical Context," *Journal of Consumer Culture* 12, no. 1 (March 2012): 67.

11 See: Nader.org, "Biographical Facts | The Nader Page," accessed November 29, 2012, http://nader.org/2006/03/01/biographical-facts/; See: Public Citizen, "About Public Citizen," accessed November 29, 2012, http://www.citizen.org/Page.aspx?pid=2306.

Act, which was passed in 2010 as a reaction to the crisis and recession of 2008.[12] This is just one example of how consumer activist NGOs may work as a form of consumer lobby in federal policy-making. On the other hand, such organizations also serve to educate consumers and provide them with the necessary information about which goods or services (e.g. financial services) are safe to purchase and which are not. As Public Citizen's slogan "Defending democracy. Resisting corporate power."[13] suggests, the organization's ultimate goal is reform, not subversion. But whereas these consumer advocacy institutions operate within the sphere of consumer capitalism, other consumer activists pursue different objectives, which may aim at more than just profound reforms: the subversion of the consumerist status quo.

In this context, it is important to note that there are two forms of consumer resistance, which Jennifer Sandlin and Jamie Callahan identify as "resistance *through* consumption" on the one hand, and "resistance *to* consumption" on the other.[14] Yet, this is not to imply that ethical consumption in general means a reduction of consumption. Even if there are cases in which one can observe a reduction of consumption, it is still far from non-consumption. Rather, one may observe a translocation of the consumption site from the free market towards an alternative market place. Now, instead of huge shopping malls, people may for instance go to swap meets, thrift stores and flea markets or shop eBay, and people who direct their consumption activity at such alternatives for ethical (or lifestyle) reasons, are usually not desperately in need. What also can be observed in this case is that production issues are virtually absent, as people purchase items

---

12 Public Citizen, "Public Citizen Accomplishments," accessed November 28, 2012, http://www.citizen.org/Page.aspx?pid=2307; See also: U.S Library of Congress, Congressional Research Service, *The Dodd-Frank Wall Street Reform and Consumer Protection Act: Regulations to Be Issued by the Consumer Financial Protection Bureau*, by Curtis W. Copeland, CRS Report R41380 (Washington, DC: Office of Congressional Information and Publishing, August 25, 2010), 2.

13 Public Citizen, "Public Citizen Home Page," accessed November 29, 2012, http://www.citizen.org/Page.aspx?pid=183.

14 See: Jennifer A. Sandlin and Jamie L. Callahan, "Deviance, Dissonance, and Détournement," *Journal of Consumer Culture* 9, no. 1 (March 2009): 89.

that have been in use before and therefore consumption does not take place in a branded retail environment as would be the case with the purchase of brand-new apparel or shoes.

4.2 Consumption as Civic Participation

When it comes to food, however, the situation is slightly different, since the production aspect cannot be ignored the way it is in second-hand buying. However, the shift to alternative niche markets can also be observed here, when, for example, consumers visit local farmer markets or fair trade stores instead of supermarkets. Therefore, resistance to consumption still has to be regarded in terms of consumption; albeit in a reduced volume, consumption shifts to niche markets. The resulting redirection of the cash flow away from the large companies and retailers towards smaller, specialized market segments may be observed in almost all forms of alternative consumption – especially in those that do not primarily promote a downshift of people's consumption activity. The idea of "voting with your dollar"[15] is particularly present in the ethical niche markets. Therefore, consumption, meaning the purchase of fairly and/or sustainably produced consumer goods, which in the majority of cases involves certain ethical and political considerations, may be looked upon as a form political participation.

The inherently problematic concept of the citizen-consumer must be brought into play again. It is problematic for two reasons; first, there is the long-standing dichotomy between the public and private spheres in American culture. Whereas the former may be regarded as the traditionally male dominated domain of politics, the latter used to be the preserve of women, whose acts of consumption were limited to the family and the household. But, regardless of the fact that these distinctions between the gender roles have, by and large, been blurred since the 1950s, the private-public dichotomy has persisted. Instead of a gendered role allocation, the opposition between self-interest and public interest remains a central issue. Because of this "ideological contradiction"[16] between consumerism and citizenship, consumption and political action are sometimes still regarded

---

15   Johnston, "The Citizen-Consumer Hybrid," 230.
16   Ibid., 231.

as mutually exclusive. Secondly, the blurring of the lines between politics and economics, which followed neoliberal policy-making when the market increasingly became an arena for consumer politics, the citizen-consumers' attention was directed "[...] toward market rather than state actors."[17]

But, to simply equate the consumer with the citizen[18] is not sufficient to resolve these contradictions. Therefore, Michele Micheletti breaks the concept of the citizen-consumer down to what she calls "*individualized collective action*" – a concept which not only "[...] combines self-interest and the general good" but also allows for a more precise account of "[...] the political landscape changes of postmodernization"[19] and their impact on the market. Furthermore, this concept of "individualized collective action," which is based on the assumption of a self-reflexive and self-assertive consumer who gets directly involved in what Micheletti calls "active subpolitics," outlines a setting in which "[r]esponsibility is not delegated to leaders and officials, it is taken personally and jointly."[20] Consumption, as Linda Neilson and Pamela Paxton contend, "[...] is not a wholly individualistic endeavor. Instead, consumer behavior is embedded in social relations."[21] Thereby, by putting strong emphasis on social capital, which they describe as "a combination of trust and formal/informal social associations," they argue that political consumerism does not just take place on an individual level. Rather, as the authors contend, social capital, which may manifest itself in particular kinds of networks, "[...] will influence political consumerism by influencing an individual's access to information about opportunities to politically consume and their motivation to do so."[22]

The public-private and individual-collective dichotomies are not only a theoretical problem – though Micheletti at least in part resolves this problem with her concept of "individualized collective action"– for it can be found in the ideological discourse of consumer activism as well. That

---

17   Micheletti, *Political Virtue and Shopping*, 17.
18   This is what Michael Schudson suggests, when he equates consumer choice with political choice. See above: chapter 2.2.1, 17.
19   Micheletti, *Political Virtue and Shopping*, 25.
20   Ibid., 27 Fig. 1.1.
21   Neilson and Paxton, "Social Capital and Political Consumerism," 7.
22   Ibid., 9.

is why Josée Johnston advises against a rash acceptance of this "simplistic dichotomy between consumer dupes versus consumer heroes."[23] However, in the praxis of consumer activism this simple contrast turns out to be a defining factor of consumer movements. As Robert Kozinets and Jay Handelman demonstrate, it is exactly this dualistic stereotypy, which is reflected in some activists' view of their contemporary consumers. According to this perspective, "[t]he activist is portrayed as both more knowledgeable than the stereotyped consumer and as morally superior to him or her."[24] This "evangelical orientation,"[25] as the authors term it, gets all the more pronounced the more radical a movement is.

Ethical and political consumption in many cases does not necessarily involve such radicalization. Especially when it comes to everyday acts of consumption such as grocery shopping, which according to Josée Johnston, "[...] is not simply a banal, private concern, but represents a key private public nexus, as well as a potential entry-point to political engagement."[26] Therefore, the politicization of consumer choice has to be seen as something that occurs within the market, and does not necessarily bring about radical positions like advocating to opt out of consumerism. In fact, most of the effects of political and ethical consumption do occur within the boundaries of the market. This most certainly does not make consumers less ethical, because one may still assume that people make deliberate choices for ethical and/or political reasons without having to escape or withdraw from the market.

4.3 Targeting Corporations and the Quest for Alternatives

Exploitive methods and the lack of transparency in the production process are among the main reasons why large, multinational corporations have been increasingly under fire by consumer activism during the last two decades. The discontent with the big players in the world market has caused numerous consumers to resort to market segments that provide alternatives. Especially the food and garment industries have been at

---

23   Johnston, "The Citizen-Consumer Hybrid," 234.
24   Kozinets and Handelman, "Adversaries of Consumption," 699.
25   Ibid., 700.
26   Johnston, "The Citizen-Consumer Hybrid," 239.

the center of most consumer activist criticism since the 1990s. The various consumer movements that have been emerging over the last two or three decades are often "[...] portrayed as organized around goals that resist particular industrial or marketing practices,"[27] as Kozinets and Handelman put it. However, in many cases, the agendas of ethical and political consumerism may reach far beyond the sphere of consumption itself; they include environmental issues, human rights issues, and politics.

Contemporary forms of ethical and political consumption, as well as consumer activism, reflect a shift "from formal politics to consumer politics."[28] This is evocative of Naomi Klein's aforementioned metaphor of 'the modern town square.' Historically, town squares – like the archetypal Roman forum – were open spaces for public gatherings and political debates. But today, it seems, not much has remained of this kind of civic culture, since brands have come to pervade everyday life and politics. In this way, the cultural and political landscape of America may be regarded as a uniform "brandscape"[29] in which increasingly powerful corporations have assumed the role of the policy makers, and, therefore, much of the people's political action is directed at these corporations' brands. Bryant Simon identifies this as a "[...] transfer of power from the government to corporations, which is a hallmark of the emerging global neo-liberal order," and sees therein the reason why many "protestors have decided to focus on brands rather than on policy makers to get things done."[30] Kalle Lasn, one of the most outspoken contemporary consumer activists, even proclaims: "America is no longer a country. It's a multitrillion-dollar brand."[31] And, indeed, as the government's leverage over the neoliberal market seems to be ever shrinking, whereas the corporations' political authority is constantly growing, it seems as if the consumer's role is essentially that of a voter.

In fact, the political dimension of consumption is not merely a matter of choice; it is primarily a matter of making oneself heard. Choice, as an act

---

27   Kozinets and Handelman, "Adversaries of Consumption," 691.
28   Simon, "Not Going to Starbucks," 147.
29   Heath and Potter, *Nation of Rebels*, 238.
30   Simon, "Not Going to Starbucks," 147.
31   Kalle Lasn, *Culture Jam: How to Reverse America's Suicidal Consumer Binge, and Why We Must* (New York: Quill, 2000), xii.

of voting, would then be a postpositioned secondary dimension, a means of asserting consumer interest. In this context, boycotts are the most widespread means of making consumer choice political. Moreover, America's long history of boycotts has proven this special form of consumer behavior to be the most effective. Therefore, boycotting has remained the most prominent means of exerting pressure on corporations among activists, as well as ethical and political consumers. The use of boycotts is manifold as various consumer movements with various goals use it as means to an end. Furthermore, what probably makes boycotting an even more powerful leverage is that it often occurs in conjunction with forms of "positive political consumerism," to borrow Michele Micheletti's term. Positive buying, or "buycotts" – as opposed to boycotting, which she terms "negative political consumerism" – means that the consumer does not entirely withdraw their buying power from the market but channels it towards alternative products and brands.[32] Consequently, the niches, which profit the most from this redirection of the cash flow, are allowed to grow. Therefore, what is commonly referred to as boycotts does not necessarily mean a reduction of consumption rather it also includes positive political consumerism. In any case, one may observe a considerable impact especially when boycotts are involved, as Jill Klein et al. find: "As a result of greater public attention to corporate social responsibility and the increased vulnerability of brands and corporate reputations, boycotts have become ever more relevant for management decision making."[33]

In a time in which more and more companies have become global players in the market, the political implications – whether local, national, or global – of boycotts may be immense.[34] At the center of many boycotts and buycotts are issues of corporate behavior, or rather misbehavior, and the societal impact thereof. Corporate social responsibility was, according to David Vogel, already an issue that came up with the Civil Rights

---

32 See: Micheletti, *Political Virtue and Shopping*, 80.
33 Jill Gabrielle Klein, N. Craig Smith, and Andrew John, "Why We Boycott: Consumer Motivations for Boycott Participation," *Journal of Marketing* 68, no. 3 (July 2004): 92.
34 See: Simon, "Not Going to Starbucks," 153ff; Klein, Smith, and John, "Why We Boycott," 92.

Movement[35] in the 1960s when corporations were increasingly held responsible "[...] for the welfare of the communit[ies] in which [they were] located." But what had begun as a plain demand on local businesses to hire African Americans, to increase the public good of local communities, would soon reveal a potential to shift "[...] from the local to the national level."[36] Thus, being "[...] a source of consumer power and a mechanism for the social control of business, boycotts also have public policy implications."[37] With the emergence of environmentalism increasing the range of topics among consumer activism, and neoliberalism eventually spawning a whole range of new issues, which came about with the outsourcing of production to low-wage countries, the calls for corporate social responsibility have been growing ever louder. Today, however, the issues for which corporations are held responsible exceed matters of community welfare. Brands and corporations are targeted around a variety of other issues, such as deficiencies in the treatment of workers, unethical treatment of animals, environmental issues, and even the political involvement of the corporations themselves. In other words, the issues reach from a local to a global scale.

At times, corporations are even targeted for taking, or not taking, a stance on certain political issues. Bryant Simon exemplifies this in the case of Starbucks, which has repeatedly been the target of consumer activism. On the level of local politics, Starbucks is of course just one of many examples of brands[38] which have been repeatedly criticized for their business practices. The expansion of large chains, like Starbucks franchises, is generally held responsible for driving smaller, local businesses out of the market.[39]

---

35   At this point, it has to be noted that the Civil Rights Movement was first and foremost a social and political movement and not a consumer movement. Even though civil rights activists utilized means of marked based pressure to achieve their ends.

36   Vogel, "Tracing the American Roots of the Political Consumerism Movement," 85f.

37   Klein, Smith, and John, "Why We Boycott," 92.

38   Other examples for large chain stores and franchises are Blockbuster video stores, the Gap, or the Body Shop. All of which were at least once were in the center of consumer activist critique. See: Klein, No Logo, 131.

39   See: Simon, "Not Going to Starbucks," 153.

The result, Klein laments, is a clone-like environment.[40] But whereas this seems to be a quite consistent matter, on national and global levels there are other examples of how consumer politics interfere with corporate behavior issues, which one might not necessarily expect to be interconnected. For instance, Simon brings in the example of gun control, an issue which one might think hardly relates to Starbucks. But in 2010 Starbucks was targeted by consumer activists "[…] to test a Washington state law that allowed gun owners to openly carry weapons in public places, that is, if the stores let them do so."[41] As Simon further explains, Starbucks biggest fault was simply its hesitation in taking a position in this debate while other restaurant chains rather quickly responded by declaring that they would not welcome gun carriers.

An example from the late 1990s demonstrates how this kind of consumer politics can also have a global impact. At that time, Starbucks' opening of shops in Israel "[…] fuelled pro-Palestinian enmity towards [the] company," especially in America and large parts of the Western world.[42] Starbucks gave in to market pressure, and the sheer violence emanating from the protests against the World Trade Organization, which had turned into a full-blown riot with the vandalization of the shops of various multinational corporations in Seattle. However, as soon as Starbucks retreated from Israel, in response to the boycott campaign of pro-Palestinian groups, it incurred the anger of pro-Israeli groups. Since then the company, which still operates shops in the Arabic countries of the Middle East, has been walking a tightrope; the difficulty is that there is often only a thin line between business decisions and political decisions.[43] This eventuates in the question of to what extent the company could or should be involved in global political issues that just incidentally relate to product or brand focused consumer politics. However, there is no simple answer to that question for they may vary from case to case, and the degree to which apparently plain business decisions

---

40   See: Klein, *No Logo*, 131f.
41   Simon, "Not Going to Starbucks," 155.
42   Ibid., 158; see also: Stanley Holmes, "Planet Starbucks," *Businessweek*, September 8, 2002, http://www.businessweek.com/stories/2002-09-08/planet-starbucks.
43   See: Simon, "Not Going to Starbucks," 159.

may evoke serious political repercussions on the side of the consumer, which may be disruptive to the company's success. Hence, the case of Starbucks is an excellent example which shows that to consume is – more than ever – to make a political statement, and that consumers increasingly expect corporations to do the same.

In 'traditional' consumer politics, such as fair trade buying, anti-sweatshop activism, green consumerism, environmentally oriented or sustainable consumption, similar local, national and global dimensions can also be observed. However, one will find that many issues that may have been associated with specific movements, like anti-sweatshop, more often than not, converge with the agendas of other consumer movements. For instance, whereas the anti-sweatshop movement pursues rather globally oriented goals, such as the improvement of the poor labor conditions in low-wage countries or bans on child labor, green consumerism focuses on issues that aim at making both a domestic/national impact, and also a global impact. Most common are issues of sustainability as related to the industrial pollution of air and water in America and abroad, or the destruction of rainforests. In fact, certain aspects of green consumerism, like the consumption of organic food, may be remarkably focused on the local community. The consumers' rejection of what Michael Pollan describes as the "corn based food chain" – the large-scale food industries, whose products often contain genetically engineered crops – in favor of "grass based food chain," which is made up of small scale, local, farmers, who directly sell their (organic) products to the consumer[44] and may sometimes involve strong anti-globalization sentiments.[45] The underlying idea is that the consumers want to know the origin of the products and food they consume.

This idea also underlies the fair trade movement, which may be seen as situated somewhere in between, for it embraces human rights as well as environmental issues on global and domestic levels. Fair trade organizations advertise their products by promoting aspects like the decent payment of farmers and workers, and organic, shade grown and "bird-friendly"

---

44   See: Michael Pollan, *The Omnivore's Dilemma: A Natural History of Four Meals* (New York: Penguin Press, 2006), 239.
45   See: Ibid., 255.

coffee,[46] for which no rainforests need to be cut down. Thus, it is rather obvious why the fair trade sector appeals to ethical consumers, and it is steadily growing. The *Fair Trade Federation Trends Report* released in 2009 stated that, of all Fair Trade Organizations in the United States, 78,4% of them are for-profit businesses, and the wholesale and importing branch grew immensely to 81% of the entire fair trade sector.[47] But not only fair trade companies, also "green" companies in general, registered considerable growth rates in the 2000s. An A. T. Kearney market analysis titled *"Green" Winners*, which was published in 2009, reveals how "sustainability-focused companies," be it the food, automobile or technology industries, have not only survived the financial crisis of 2008 but even gained value.[48]

Since this ethical niche is far from being a marginal phenomenon in the consumer market, it is hardly surprising that other companies and corporations have discovered the appeal of the ethical market. Thus, in order to attract a certain kind of ethically and politically involved customer, businesses of all kinds pose as model corporate citizens. And again Starbucks is a classic example. On its official website, Starbucks claims to be "a responsible company" and puts great emphasis on the company's additional value derived from its ethically and socially responsible behavior. Starbucks offers a long list of topics to which the company is dedicated, and it almost covers the whole range of issues frequently raised by consumer activists. Just to mention a few examples, Starbucks makes the case for community involvement, such as creating jobs, environmental aspects like the reduction of waste, and even climate change and fair trade. As of 2011, the company is even listed on the Forbes list of *The World's Most Ethical Companies*, among 110 "model corporate citizens" including

---

46   See: Green America, "Greener Coffee - Green America's Responsible Shopper," *Greenamerica.org*, accessed December 5, 2012, http://www.greenamerica.org/programs/responsibleshopper/live/coffee.cfm.

47   See: Fair Trade Federation, *Report on Trends in the North American Fair Trade Market* (Washington, DC: Fair Trade Federation, March 2009), 4, www.fairtradefederation.org.

48   See: Daniel Mahler et al., *Green Winners: The Performance of Sustainability-focused Companies During the Financial Crisis* (Chicago: A.T. KEARNEY, 2009), http://www.atkearney.com/de/paper/-/asset_publisher/dVxv4Hz2h-8bS/content/green-winners/10192.

other big players like Whole Foods Market, and General Mills and PepsiCo – both of which one might not necessarily expect to see on such a list.[49] While critics might not necessarily agree with this list, this shows the difficulty of measuring ethical corporate behavior or corporate social responsibility.

One of the biggest problems is that there is no standard definition of what qualifies companies as ethical and socially responsible businesses. One simply has to take a look at the wide variety of fair trade organizations and labeling schemes. But even though Starbucks, by its own account, purchases 86% of all its coffee from sources which produce and trade according to the standards agreed upon by various fair trade organizations,[50] Fran Hawthorne finds that the company's "[...] standards don't specifically forbid child labor, forced labor or discrimination." She further argues, that the company's "[...] efforts speak more to ensuring the quality of beans [...] than the quality of farmers' lives."[51] After all, Starbucks is still a profit-oriented multinational corporation, but the ethical attitude seems to serve the company's success.

Aside from Starbucks, other companies, especially food retailers, have also cultivated a similar ethical appeal, like, for instance, the Texas-based Whole Foods Market. Forbes lists this company, which has a market value of $ 15,7 billion, among "America's most trustworthy companies."[52] With near 310 stores in the United States, Canada, and the United Kingdom, Whole Foods Market is one of the major occupants of the organic foods niche. The company's "green mission" covers every major aspect of green sustainable consumerism, reaching from healthy, genetically unmodified foods, up to investing in alternative energies in order to cover as much of

---

49   See: Jacquelyn Smith, "The World's Most Ethical Companies," *Forbes.com*, March 15, 2011, http://www.forbes.com/2011/03/15/most-ethical-companies-leadership-responsibility-ethisphere.html.

50   See: Starbucks, "Responsibly Grown and Fair Trade Coffee," accessed December 5, 2012, http://www.starbucks.com/responsibility/sourcing/coffee.

51   Fran Hawthorne, *Ethical Chic: The Inside Story of the Companies We Think We Love* (Boston: Beacon Press, 2012), 55.

52   Jacquelyn Smith, "America's Most Trustworthy Companies," *Forbes.com*, March 20, 2012, http://www.forbes.com/sites/jacquelynsmith/2012/03/20/americas-most-trustworthy-companies/2/.

the individual stores energy consumption with wind and solar powered as possible.[53] Delivering the full package of social and ethical responsibility, Whole Foods success seems to prove it right. The image of Trader Joe's, the major competitor of Whole Foods,[54] is also fashioned in a similar ethical manner. But even though the company sets "stringent 'natural' and 'green' standards" for its private-label goods, which make for 80% of its product range, there are no standards for the products from other labels that Trader Joe's offers for sale.[55] However, unlike Whole Foods, Trader Joe's, which specializes in international, exotic products, does not advertise its green image overtly. In fact, the company received a rather poor overall rating of 3.6 and an average product rating of 4.7 out of 10 possible points by GoodGuide.com.[56]

Thus, Trader Joe's, which advertises itself as "your neighborhood store," probably profits more from its exotic appeal than from its ethical appeal. Even though the company abides by the *California Transparency in Supply Chains Act of 2010*,[57] supports the ban on forced or child labor, and shows some neighborhood involvement by donating food to "fight hunger,"[58] this cannot hide fact that the Trader Joe's has large deficiencies in terms of environmental sustainability. But, occupying the exotic niche with an ethical overtone seems to be Trader Joe's formula for success. Due to putting less emphasis on organic production and fair trade than Whole Foods, for example, Trader Joe's has in fact been the target

---

53   See: Whole Foods Market, "Green Mission," accessed December 5, 2012, http://www.wholefoodsmarket.com/mission-values/environmental-steward-ship/green-mission.

54   See: Walter Loeb, "Aldi's Trader Joe's is a Winner," *Forbes.com*, May 17, 2012, http://www.forbes.com/sites/walterloeb/2012/05/17/aldis-trader-joes-is-a-winner/3/.

55   See: Hawthorne, *Ethical Chic*, 108.

56   The average product rating is made up of 6.8 Health, 3.6 Environment, and 3.7 Society. See: GoodGuide.com, "Trader Joe's Ratings & Reviews | Best & Worst Products | GoodGuide," accessed December 6, 2012, http://www.goodguide.com/brands/124947-trader-joes.

57   See: Trader Joe's, "Customer Updates," accessed December 5, 2012, http://www.traderjoes.com/about/customer-updates-responses.asp?i=80.

58   Trader Joe's, "Neighborhood Involvement" Trader Joe's, accessed December 5, 2012, http://www.traderjoes.com/stores/neighborhood-involvement.asp.

of environmental activism in the past. For instance, the company had issues with Greenpeace regarding sustainable seafood, and, consequently, Trader Joe's agreed to ban all seafood that is not sourced from sustainable fishing from its assortment by the end of 2012.[59] But it has never been targeted to such the extent that other companies, like Starbucks, have been. This may be due at least in part to the sheer difference in the companies' sizes. Trader Joe's operates only a little more than 360 stores throughout the U.S., exclusively,[60] as opposed to the roughly 17.000 Starbucks Shops worldwide. Besides, the fact that Trader Joe's targets at a very specific and exclusive group of customers makes it tactically useless in the pursuit of larger political goals by means of market based pressure. Therefore, Fran Hawthorne alleges that the company, which only offers a limited selection of largely exotic foods, and thereby draws only a rather small but affluent clientele, is being elitist. She further argues that by putting "[t]he focus on exotic food [...] Trader Joe's has created a false demand for unnecessary consumption," but neither that nor the deficient record of sustainability "[...] seem to bother consumer activists."[61] This, and the fact that Trader Joe's never really been under fire by consumer activism, may suggest the assumption that a good portion of consumer activists may be classed among that kind of customers who are frequenters of Trader Joe's. The question of who constitutes the group of consumer activists within the American society will be discussed below.

Given the various forms of consumer activism, of which environment-related issues labor-related issues are only two – though certainly the most central dimensions – one will find that there is hardly anything that could be described as a coherent agenda, and much less a distinctive movement. It is similarly difficult, if not impossible, to find alternatives with nothing

---

59 See: Hawthorne, *Ethical Chic*, 109; Greenpeace, "Trader Joe's Gets a Little Greener," March 29, 2010, http://www.greenpeace.org/usa/en/news-and-blogs/news/trader-joe-greener/.

60 However, it is important to note that unlike Whole Foods Market, which is an independent corporation, Trader Joe's is a subsidiary of German Aldi Nord, a privately owned multinational company with about 5.081 stores in different European Countries plus the 367 Trader Joe's branches in the United States. See also: Loeb, "Aldi's Trader Joe's Is a Winner."

61 Hawthorne, *Ethical Chic*, 119.

to be faulted. However, food retailers, which exhibit a relatively high level of corporate responsibility, like Whole Foods Market, seem to profit from the generally increasing ethical and environmental awareness, even among those who are less likely to take part in boycotts. But, at the same time, Whole Foods is a multi-billion dollar enterprise which, even though it is located in the ethical niche, also has a mainstream appeal. Josée Johnston and Michelle Szabo for instance find that "[t]he store draws a larger number of buyers than small-scale 'ethical' venues, and offers many products that appeal to a wider swath of the shopping public, and not only to deeply committed food activists."[62] Therefore, Whole Foods Market probably would not have been so successful if it was not for this mainstream appeal.

Today, the supermarket has become a space for consumer politics of all kinds, especially since the practice of "[b]oycotting has [...] become institutionalized and more globalized."[63] No matter what the particular objectives may be, "boycotts are about leverage and about being heard; they are about the practice of political power."[64] And since this form of market-based pressure may lead to serious repercussions for brands and corporations, "marketers prefer to avoid [such situations]" because, as Jill Klein et al. remark, they could "[...] [provide] shoppers with reasons to try competitors' products."[65] Therefore, corporations may be well advised to react to boycott campaigns otherwise, as the case of Nestlé has shown, a corporation might risk severe long-term damage to its corporate and brand images, which may be overcome only with great difficulty.

4.4 Who are the Alternative Consumers?

Since there is no coherent consumer movement today, the answer to the question of which people are the most likely to engage themselves in ethical and political consumerism and to which social group they belong is not as simple as it might seem at first. Due to the shortage of quantitative

---

62   Josée Johnston and Michelle Szabo, "Reflexivity and the Whole Foods Market Consumer: The Lived Experience of Shopping for Change," *Agriculture and Human Values* 28, no. 3 (September 2011): 304.

63   Micheletti, *Political Virtue and Shopping*, 82.

64   Simon, "Not Going to Starbucks," 152.

65   Klein, Smith, and John, "Why We Boycott," 105f.

empirical data derived from comprehensive analyses, most approaches on ethical and political consumer behavior rely on qualitative small-scale case studies conducted among a small sample of the population, on the basis of which, interpretations regarding the demographics of ethical and political consumerism are made. However, it must be noted that most of these qualitative studies can hardly be considered representative of the entire population. Notwithstanding, literature on this topic generally suggests that ethical and political consumption is more likely to occur among the inhabitants of the more affluent sections of society. Yet, "[o]n empirical grounds," as Josée Johnston et al. remark, "scholars lack data demonstrating that privileged populations necessarily think more deeply about food ethics, even though they have resources to buy more 'ethical' products."[66] Nevertheless, the interpretation of available data and (socio-historical) facts allows for relatively accurate characterization of the ethical consumer – though, to be sure, this can only be an ideal type that is yet to be proven.

For instance, David Brooks' "Bobos," or Heath and Potter's "rebel consumers," being the posterity of the process of social, cultural and economic transformation of the 1960s and 1970s, are the most prevalent in alternative lifestyles. As mentioned above, these groups, whom Brooks refers to as "countercultural capitalists,"[67] belong to the middle to upper sections of society, which have rather high incomes, high levels of education and a comparatively large volume of cultural capital.[68] And, as Friedland et al. state, this is the group where one will find "the individuals who most engage in civic and political life"[69] – and thus in forms of alternative consumption and consumer activism. What also contributes to supporting this interpretation is the fact that ethical shopping alternatives tend to be more readily available in areas whose population exhibits the aforementioned characteristics. Ethical shopping alternative may therefore be compared to Fred Hirsch's theory of positional goods, which was discussed in chapter

---

66   Josée Johnston, Michelle Szabo, and Alexandra Rodney, "Good Food, Good People: Understanding the Cultural Repertoire of Ethical Eating," *Journal of Consumer Culture* 11, no. 3 (March 18, 2011): 294.
67   Brooks, *Bobos in Paradise*, 110.
68   See also the discussion of positional goods above: chapter 2.3.2, 36ff.
69   Friedland et al., "Capital, Consumption, Communication, and Citizenship," 38.

two. As Johnston et al. find: "Many of the shopping and eating spaces articulating a discourse of ethical consumption, such as Whole Foods Market, are positioned to serve economic elites."[70] Apart from the issue of local availability "[...] market research generally suggests that cost is a major barrier to participation in ethical consumption markets."[71] Hence, on the one hand one can observe a rather limited physical availability of ethical shopping alternatives, which is one qualifier of a positional good, and, on the other hand, one may also notice a certain 'social limitation'[72] inherent to ethical and political consumption. Since not every consumer shares the same dispositions necessary to buy ethically, and cultural capital also plays a certain role, there is a high probability that alternative consumption is the reserve of a rather small 'elite' seen in relation to the rest of the American consumer society. But, nevertheless, to assume that ethical consumption is exclusively a matter of economic privilege would be a mistake. Even though less privileged groups are mostly "weakly or moderately engaged" this does not make them automatically "[...] 'unethical' in their consumption practices."[73] Johnston et al. further observe that, within the upper middle class, the way in which "[...] they [position] themselves in relation to other people" plays an important role as "[...] the idea of healthful, high-quality foods providing a sense of cultural distinction or status." Therefore, "[...] higher class people draw symbolic boundaries based on cultural distinctions more than lower class people because they have more cultural capital."[74]

Regarding age and gender, Michele Micheletti contends that "[...] political consumerism has been shown to be connected to the citizen agency of young people and women."[75] Even though not much research has been done on young people's involvement in consumer politics, she argues that this could be explained with "[...] the appeal of lifestyle politics among the youth, trends toward individualization, and their tendency to

---

70 Johnston, Szabo, and Rodney, "Good Food, Good People," 294.
71 Ibid., 296.
72 See above: chapter 2.3, 36f.
73 Johnston, Szabo, and Rodney, "Good Food, Good People," 307, 311.
74 Ibid., 312.
75 Micheletti, *Political Virtue and Shopping*, 17.

find the formal political sphere alienating."[76] In contrast, several reasons for women's involvement in ethical and political consumerism or consumer politics may be seen as the result of historically established cultural and political traditions. Therefore, women's significant presence in the realm of alternative consumerism today[77] may be due to the "traditional sex role" of "women as family shoppers" being responsible for the health and well-being of the family.[78] Furthermore, as "[...] women have historically been excluded from institutions of the public sphere"[79] they have been pioneering the field of consumer politics, at least since the early twentieth century, as was already discussed. In the past, women's involvement in the market had laid the foundations for the political empowerment of women. Even though, the gender specific roles in terms of consumption might not have ceased to exist, it would be a misconception to regard political consumption as an exclusively female domain.

4.5 Culture Jamming – A Special Case of Consumer Activism

Apart from the politicization of everyday consumer practices, such as food shopping, some consumer activist movements have cultivated a rather creative method of consumer resistance called culture jamming. This special form of market-based activism "[...] differs considerably from conventional modes of political participation,"[80] because culture jamming does not necessarily involve an act of consumption. Rather than "resistance *through* consumption," as it is the case with most of the abovementioned examples,

---

76 Micheletti, *Political Virtue and Shopping*, 17.
77 See: Neilson and Paxton, "Social Capital and Political Consumerism," 10f.
78 See: Michele Micheletti, "Why More Women? Issues of Gender and Political Consumerism," in *Politics, Products, and Markets: Exploring Political Consumerism Past and Present* (New Brunswick, NJ: Transaction Publishers, 2009), 225.
79 Micheletti, *Political Virtue and Shopping*, 18.
80 Jonah Peretti and Michele Micheletti, "The Nike Sweatshop Email: Political Consumerism, Internet, and Culture Jamming," in *Politics, Products, and Markets: Exploring Political Consumerism Past and Present*, ed. Michele Micheletti, Andreas Follesdal, and Dietlind Stolle (New Brunswick, NJ: Transaction Publishers, 2009), 136.

culture jamming predominantly propagates "resistance *to* consumption."[81] Hence, as Michele Micheletti puts it, "[t]he purpose of these actions is to challenge the expensive image-making process by making the politics of products visible to the global consumer."[82] This means that culture jammers directly attack the brand image rather than using conventional techniques of alternative consumerism. Kozinets and Handelman call this "anti-advertising activism,"[83] and this ambition is particularly reflected in the names of movements such as the Billboard Liberation Front or Adbusters. Culture jamming, which is essentially about the alteration and parody of corporate advertising messages and brand image campaigns, draws on the subcultural repertoire, which may be observed in the use of street art. This particular technique may also be called "subvertising."[84] This "ad hoc form of social marketing,"[85] as Vince Carducci calls it, aims at one specific goal, namely to "promote anti-consumerism."[86] In this context, Kalle Lasn, the founder of Adbusters, introduces the pregnant term "meme war," wherein the media is the battleground. Therefore, Lasn sees culture jamming as *the* driving force in the fight for a "free information environment" not corrupted by brands.[87]

Culture jamming, according to Vince Carducci, "[...] can be seen as a form of consumer boycott."[88] In that context he mentions Buy Nothing Day[89] which was originally initiated by Adbusters, and which takes place annually on Black Friday after Thanksgiving. This day, which traditionally marks the start of the Christmas shopping season, and is when retailers

---

81 Sandlin and Callahan, "Deviance, Dissonance, and Détournement," 89.

82 Micheletti, *Political Virtue and Shopping*, 14.

83 Kozinets and Handelman, "Adversaries of Consumption," 693.

84 Sandlin and Callahan, "Deviance, Dissonance, and Détournement," 91, 97; See also: Vince Carducci, "Culture Jamming: A Sociological Perspective," *Journal of Consumer Culture* 6, no. 1 (March 2006): 124; Kozinets and Handelman, "Adversaries of Consumption," 698.

85 Carducci, "Culture Jamming," 119.

86 Ibid., 131.

87 See: Lasn, *Culture Jam*, 123f, 127.

88 Carducci, "Culture Jamming," 131.

89 See: Adbusters Media Foundation, "Buy Nothing Day + Buy Nothing Christmas #OCCUPYXMAS | Adbusters Culturejammer Headquarters," accessed December 10, 2012, http://www.adbusters.org/campaigns/bnd.

lure customers in with bargains and special offers, is used by Adbusters to convey their message to stop consuming for one day. Hence, in a way, this could be described as a boycott taking aim at consumer capitalism in general. However, in this case, simply to argue that North Americans consume too much will probably not suffice as a basis for developing a broad consumer movement. Besides, the frequent use of anti-capitalistic vocabulary is probably more likely to attract anarchists[90] rather than ordinary consumers. Therefore, it is helpful to look at culture jammers' favorite adversary – Nike. Nike is a corporation which has been targeted by almost every single kind of consumer activism throughout at least the last two decades. The company's powerful brand image, marketing tactics, and its non-transparent modes of production make for an ideal target for consumer activism, and especially culture jamming. The "Swoosh," Nike's virtually omnipresent logo, had become the "swooshtika."[91]

At the very forefront of the anti-Nike movement are the Vancouver-based culture jammers of Adbusters, who published a series of Nike spoof or "unswooshing"[92] ads, which are a prime example of the tactics of culture jamming. But Adbusters went even further by launching its own sneaker line called "Blackspot Shoes." The whole endeavor is meant as a potshot at Nike. However, with only two models available, one of which is the so-called "Unswoosher,"[93] Blackspot sneakers, which are made from natural and recycled materials and manufactured in Pakistan by "unionized workers" under fair labor conditions, may hardly be considered serious competition to Nike, but rather as a statement against the corporation. Another example

---

90   See: Laura Portwood-Stacer, "Anti-consumption as Tactical Resistance: Anarchists, Subculture, and Activist Strategy," *Journal of Consumer Culture* 12, no. 1 (March 2012): 101. The author's findings also suggest that this is a tactic which is deliberately employed by activist to (symbolically) distance themselves from the mainstream.

91   See: Klein, *No Logo*, 367.

92   Adbusters Media Foundation, "Unswooshing | Adbusters Culturejammer Headquarters," accessed November 27, 2012, http://www.adbusters.org/spoofads/unswooshing.

93   Adbusters Media Foundation, "Blackspot Shoes | Adbusters Culturejammer Headquarters," accessed December 10, 2012, http://www.adbusters.org/campaigns/blackspot.

that, unexpectedly, found a wide resonance among culture jammers is Jonah Peretti's infamous 2001 *Nike Sweatshop Email*. Starting as a culture jamming experiment, Peretti's email correspondence with Nike about his request to have the word 'sweatshop' printed on a pair of Nike iD shoes which was ultimately declined by the company[94] would eventually go viral after he forwarded these emails to a couple of his friends. This shows how the Internet has become an important means of communication and dissemination of information among consumer activists.

Another important tactic of culture jamming is the use of emotion in order to mobilize consumers.[95] As Sandlin and Callahan point out, emotions may serve "[...] as a means to generate collective action."[96] The authors further elaborate two distinct dimensions of emotion in culture jamming. The first, targeting *"audience emotions,"* is the external dimension of a movement's "emotional culture." It is the "[...] attempt to shake consumers out of their perceived false sense of emotional harmony by confronting them with symbols and activities causing emotional dissonance."[97] Adbusters' TV spot to advertise Buy Nothing Day is such an example; it portrays the lot of American consumers as a voracious pig and suggests that the world "[...] could die because of the way [the] North Americans live."[98] Even though none of the large broadcasting networks granted Adbusters airtime for the spot, it would nevertheless gain publicity through TV news and the Internet. The second internal emotional dimension providing for the cohesion of the movement is twofold. On the one hand, ritualized forms of interaction among activists provides them with a sense of solidarity, and, on the other hand, "[...] interacting with

---

94 See: Peretti and Micheletti, "The Nike Sweatshop Email," 128f.
95 This is redolent of Sennett's idea of an "intimate society" in which the mutual revelation of emotions, or rather emotional bonds between individuals, becomes a means of social cohesion and thus generates a collective personality. See above: chapter 3.2.3, 75.
96 Sandlin and Callahan, "Deviance, Dissonance, and Détournement," 86.
97 Ibid., 91, 93.
98 Adbusters Media Foundation, "Censored TV Spots | Adbusters Culturejammer Headquarters," accessed December 10, 2012, http://www.adbusters.org/abtv/censored_tv_spots.html.

individuals who occupy a lower hierarchical status position [...]" provides for a feeling of power and "positive energy."[99] The latter is exactly, what Kozinets and Handelman mean when they describe the activists as "a type of modern day Puritan."[100] However, this "evangelical orientation," as the authors describe it, is hardly motivated by religion. Rather, the authors draw parallels between Evangelicalism and consumer activism by portraying the activists' self-conception of themselves as "enlightened" people who are "morally superior" to the mass "of unseeing wrong doers."[101] Consequently, this dualistic view, which depicts consumers as the activists' opponents rather than as potential fellow campaigners, is more likely to repel average consumers from getting involved.

Apart from that, the large-scale political implications of culture jamming are widely disputed. As it is often argued, the radical, ironic, anti-capitalistic tone of culture jamming, as well as the countercultural jargon, may easily be co-opted by the mainstream. Vince Carducci recapitulates this notion with his remark that the "[...] so-called oppositional or 'counter' culture can quickly be recuperated by commercial interests and integrated back into the market system [...]."[102] Thomas Frank, for instance, also draws on this notion of co-optation when he describes how marketers in the 1960s began to "[...] make rebel subcultures their own [...]."[103] This era was not only marked by the rise of "hip consumerism" but also by the "creative revolution" as "[...] the advertising industry began to recognize non-conformity."[104] In this respect, Frank regards the transformation of Volkswagen's Beetle "from [a] Nazi car to [the] love bug" as "one of the great triumphs of American marketing."[105] Likewise, Heath and Potter discuss the theory of co-optation of subversion, which they argue is interpreted by countercultural rebels as a sign of the repressiveness of the capitalist market system.[106] However, they quickly expose the co-optation

---

99   Sandlin and Callahan, "Deviance, Dissonance, and Détournement," 95f.
100 Kozinets and Handelman, "Adversaries of Consumption," 701.
101 Ibid., 699f.
102 Carducci, "Culture Jamming," 118.
103 Frank, *The Conquest of Cool*, 9.
104 Ibid., 26f, 89.
105 Ibid., 67f.
106 See: Heath and Potter, *Nation of Rebels*, 35.

theory as a myth, because, as they argue, "[...] it's a simple mechanism of adaption."[107]

What Heath and Potter describe as the "mass-marketing of rebellion"[108] today is probably best exemplified with the Billboard Liberation Front. Interestingly, this is an example of how culture jamming itself delivers the most powerful counter argument to the co-optation theory. Founded in 1977, this group of culture jammers has evolved into an advertising agency pioneering the field of "street marketing." So far, the group has designed several official billboard advertising campaigns for big corporate clients, among them Philipp Morris and McDonalds, both of which have been the subject of major controversies. As of 2010, billboards have displayed slogans like "My Life My Death My Choice" for Philip Morris or "you have about 10,000 taste buds. kill them all." and "I'm sick of it." for McDonalds.[109] And as it turned out they did not have any major negative impacts on the corporate image.

Even though the creative potential of culture jamming may also serve the purpose of advertising – the contrary effect of the originally intended purpose – one should not underestimate the potential impact of culture jamming on other forms of consumer activism. Naomi Klein shows that this is not necessarily a contradiction, because culture jamming covers the whole range "[...] from purer-than-thou Marxist-anarchists [to people] who work in the advertising industry."[110] Therefore, the fact that Adbusters, which is located at the exact opposite end of the culture jamming spectrum, is listed among the Billboard Liberation Front's strategic partners[111] is not as odd as it first seems. Both use the exact same techniques, i.e. advertising,

---

107 Ibid., 96.
108 Ibid., 130.
109 See: Billboard Liberation Front, "Billboard Liberation Front Creative Group," accessed December 11, 2012, http://www.billboardliberation.com/clients.html. In the case of McDonalds the relevant parts in the original slogans "you have about 10,000 taste buds. use them all." and "I'm lovin' it" were simply pasted over.
110 Klein, *No Logo*, 284.
111 See: Billboard Liberation Front, "Billboard Liberation Front Creative Group," accessed December 11, 2012, http://www.billboardliberation.com/partners.html.

but with different goals. Even though this makes the "radical consumer resistance movement"[112] appear less radical, it proves that culture jamming, rather than subverting consumer capitalism, may also serve to reinforce it. Therefore, when taken alone the potential impact of the culture jamming movement may be rather tenuous, which also may in part be due to the fact that its goals are in some cases articulated too vaguely, like e.g. in the Buy Nothing Day campaign. Hence, as Carducci concludes, "[c]ulture jamming has the greatest potential to achieve a useful end as a means in service to larger movements rather than as an end in itself."[113] Thus the result is an image of culture jammers as the sidekicks of other forms of consumer activism.

4.6 Postmodernism and Alternative Consumption

The sort of consumer activism discussed in this chapter is clearly a product of the neoliberal economy. The transition from Fordism to post-Fordism spawned niche markets with an ever-greater variety of specialized goods. Now, in order to supply the segmented consumer market with goods, new ways of production had to be found so that the ever-rising amounts of consumption could be covered. This segmentation also meant an expansion of the market and new modes of production in need of cheap labor, and, before long, issues of sustainability and human rights were raised. What would become the age of the superbrand not only gave rise to a new kind of consumer, but also necessitated a new kind of activism, which, unlike Naderism, directly acted within the space of the free market rather than in formal politics, because the state could no longer be considered a reliable partner in a neoliberal market. Consequently, ethical and political consumerism has become a central part of postmodern consumer culture, which, as Douglas Holt writes, "[...] was born, paradoxically, in the 1960s counterculture that opposed corporatism of all stripes."[114] The formation and expansion of ethical niche markets, which have brought forth a number of profitable businesses, was only possible because of the

---

112 Sandlin and Callahan, "Deviance, Dissonance, and Détournement," 81.
113 Carducci, "Culture Jamming," 134.
114 Holt, "Why Do Brands Cause Trouble?" 82.

consumers' increasing awareness of environmental issues that would eventually evolve into a full-fledged movement. However, apart from sustainability issues, corporate malpractice in a variety of other fields, like e.g. corporate policies, with regard to exploitive production methods, have led to an expansion of modern consumer activism.

The close ties between postmodern consumerism and the counterculture are especially evident in contemporary ethical and political consumerism. The contemporary alternative consumer features almost every characteristic trait of the postmodern consumer, which was discussed in chapter three. First of all, the emphasis on the self and individual action, and the underlying "motivation to bring about social change"[115] by means of consumption, which is the driving force behind consumer activism, can be regarded as the consumers' contribution to the construction of social reality. Furthermore, getting involved with ethical and political consumption may also serve the purpose of "self-enhancement." When individuals in the pursuit of a specific goal start acting as a group, as is the case with boycotts, Jill Klein et al. contend that "[p]articipation enables the boycotter to boost social and personal self-esteem either by associating with a cause or group of people or simply by viewing him- or herself as a moral person."[116] Interestingly, this not only shows how closely the collective and individual dimensions of political action in the market are connected; it also shows that far from large scale political implications, consumer choice, albeit ethically or politically motivated, may be extremely self-interested, for instance when "[...] people boycott to feel good about themselves."[117]

Second, the idea of an emancipated postmodern consumer as cultural producer takes shape in modern consumer activism. This is especially apparent in the case of culture jamming. Advertisements for brands and products serve as staples for cultural production, which culture jammers use to create new meaning in different contexts by means of techniques including the alteration and parody of the original meaning. This similarly occurs in other consumer movement, though it might be less obvious than in culture jamming. But nevertheless, ethical consumers may also act as

---

115 Klein, Smith, and John, "Why We Boycott," 96.
116 Ibid., 97.
117 Ibid., 106.

cultural producers by attaching new meanings to products that exceed their mere utility by far. One example is food shopping, which Josée Johnston et al. consider "as an arena for self-expression."[118] Buying organic, therefore, is not merely a question of one's personal diet, but may also carry wider social and political implications.

However, alternative consumption also comes with costs that not every consumer is willing to pay. Jill Klein et al. label it "constrained consumption,"[119] which may especially result from boycott participation. Boycotting a certain company also means that the options are limited, and, at the same time, that it is necessary that the consumer carefully reflect on every single one of his or her purchase decisions. Especially those consumers who are not hardcore activists may tend to think twice about whether or not to engage themselves in ethical or political consumerism. Therefore, experts increasingly pay attention to what is called 'conscious consumerism.' However, this does not necessarily imply the absence of values, rather, as Miriam Pepper et al. state, "[...] socially conscious consumer behaviour [sic], like its ecological counterpart, is an expression of people's pro-social and pro-environmental values."[120] Similarly, Isabelle Szmigin et al. argue "[...] that increasingly ethical considerations are entering consumer purchase decisions [...]" but, at the same time, they identify a "disconnect" between the consumer's motivations and their actual purchase decisions.[121] Further, they argue that having to deal with this "complex decision environment" ultimately results in a certain inconsistency.[122] They describe it as follows: "While the conscious consumer wants to contribute and consume ethically, this does not rule their life and indeed for some, where it is inconvenient, they will not worry about the

---

118 Johnston, Szabo, and Rodney, "Good Food, Good People," 297.

119 Klein, Smith, and John, "Why We Boycott," 98.

120 Miriam Pepper, Tim Jackson, and David Uzzell, "An Examination of the Values That Motivate Socially Conscious and Frugal Consumer Behaviors," *International Journal of Consumer Studies* 33, no. 2 (2009): 133.

121 Isabelle Szmigin, Marylyn Carrigan, and Morven G. McEachern, "The Conscious Consumer: Taking a Flexible Approach to Ethical Behaviour," *International Journal of Consumer Studies* 33, no. 2 (March 2009): 224.

122 Ibid., 228.

inconsistencies between their attitude and their behaviour [sic]."[123] Hence, even though acts of consumption can be similar to acts of voting, not every purchase decision, even if ethically motivated, may necessarily be regarded as a political decision.

Even though alternative consumerism is no longer a marginal phenomenon, critical voices still regard "[...] ethical consumption [...] an elite social practice."[124] And it is rather unlikely that this idea will be debunked any time soon. As it was discussed in this chapter, there are many indications which underpin this theory. The fact remains, that, on the one hand, the volume of cultural capital together with a certain volume of discretionary income, are two of the very basic prerequisites needed for participation in alternative consumption. On the other hand, the consumers' access to information as well as locally available ethical shopping alternatives, as in the case of food shopping, are closely connected to that group of people who, in all likeliness, are able to afford and willing to go for these alternatives. Another important point of criticism is that especially the more radical activists are attributed a certain arrogance, as they believe to know what is best for the rest of consumer society. Some activists' sense of superiority over other consumers, which Kozinets and Handelman have compared to Puritanism, exhibits this elitist way of thinking. In this context, one might even be tempted to consent with Zygmunt Bauman's description of consumer activism as "undemocratic." However, one certainly has to disagree with him when he makes consumer activism appear as a "symptom of the growing disenchantment with politics."[125] Instead, one has to carefully distinguish between formal politics on the one hand, and market-based consumer politics on the other, because the latter is strongly pronounced in consumer activist discourses as well as in political consumerism general. Therefore, Bauman's claim that people are "consumers first, citizens second"[126] cannot be maintained for the American consumer society at large.

123 Szmigin, Carrigan, and McEachern, "The Conscious Consumer," 229.
124 Johnston, Szabo, and Rodney, "Good Food, Good People," 294.
125 Bauman, *Consuming Life*, 146, 147.
126 Ibid., 149.

Finally, one has to be aware of the fact that political and ethical consumption as it is described in this chapter must not be confused with anti-consumption – much less non-consumption. Nevertheless, there certainly are points of contact, especially among the culture jamming movement, like, for example, Adbusters' explicit goal to 'subvert' global capitalism. However, this would be more in the realm of anarchist subculture in which resistance to consumption and consumerism becomes expressed through "anti-consumption practices." However, Laura Portwood-Stacer also contends that "[...] a purely non-consumptive lifestyle is an impossible achievement for anyone."[127] Hence, anarchists and anti-consumerism in the most radical form should instead be considered a marginal phenomenon, not a driving force behind all political and ethical consumerism – even though anarchist and anti-capitalist rhetoric often resonates in many forms of consumer activism and even in advertising.

---

127 Portwood-Stacer, "Anti-consumption as Tactical Resistance," 88.

5. Conclusion

Although not every consumer choice is political by default, one has to abandon the notion of consumption as a solely private act without any political implication. In other words, purchase decisions and political choices are not necessarily mutually exclusive. Thus, one will observe a certain complexity in the concept of the 'citizen consumer,' which conceptualizes consumption as a way of civic participation. Even though the citizen and the consumer are not incompatible, the merging of both concepts does not reconcile some of the most central, and inherently contradictory, dichotomies of alternative consumption. As a matter of fact, consumption may extend from the private into the public sphere, and thus become a form collective action or behavior instead of an exclusively individual form of action, as soon as it gets a political dimension. But even the most banal consumer choice involves a social component, as discussed in chapter two. As Bourdieu contends, consumer tastes develop within in the particular social context in which an individual is situated. Thus, even though the choice is formulated by the individual consumer and takes shape in their purchase decisions, consumer choice is at the same time greatly influenced by the individuals 'conditions of existence,' to borrow Bourdieu's term. Hence, the individual must not be seen in opposition to society, just as Elias suggested. This especially holds true for postmodernism, wherein the individual is standing at the center of every social relation.

In order to find out to what extent consumer decisions may also be seen as a deliberate political choice, a theory-based conceptualization of the consumer and consumer choice was needed. This was the purpose of chapter two, which elaborated on consumer sovereignty and agency and therefore dealt with the consumer as social actor. Distinction and competitive aspects of consumerism are central to such an approach, for these aspects reveal that consumer society is anything but homogenous. Furthermore, and these are the key findings of that chapter, this helped to show that rather than being a passive and manipulated dupe, the consumer must, to a certain extent, be regarded as an agent. However, consumer agency has its limits as the consumer is certainly not the single most powerful player in the market. There are strong indications that consumer sovereignty is finite, and the consumer cannot be seen as the omnipotent sovereign of the market. Instead, the consumer's freedom of choice might be curtailed, which at the same time, however, makes the consumer a negotiator of their freedom to a far greater extent than critics may be willing to accept.

In fact, as it was shown in chapter three, the relationship between consumption and politics has a long history in the United States. However, seen in historical perspective, it was not the individual act of consumption itself standing at the center of the politicization of consumption, rather it must be regarded as a form of collective political action which was embedded in social movements, such as the Civil Rights Movement. By means of such examples, I have shown how, in the past, Americans have used market-based pressure, like boycotting, as a means to political ends. With the breakdown of Fordism and the emergent neoliberal order of the market, in other words the postmodern transition, the situation would change. Other issues that were originally not consumption-related would add new impetuses to the politicization of consumption. The emergent green consumerism then paved the way for a new kind of consumer movement. This was a novelty insofar as the market became the primary arena of consumer politics, which is the major difference to earlier forms of consumer activism like Naderism, which also aimed to keep a close eye on corporations. But the tactics of the consumer advocacy of the 1960s were different insofar as it primarily acted upon the government in order to achieve its goals in the market. Later, as a consequence of neoliberalism, consumer politics became increasingly detached from formal policy-making as the state retreated from the market, and the government largely refrained from intervening in the market.

In chapter four, which dealt with specific examples of contemporary alternative consumerism, the hypothesis that consumption may also be regarded as a form of political choice was supported. Clearly, alternative consumerism may be, in some instances, a form of civic participation, and yet it cannot be overlooked that, as critics argue, modern ethical and political consumerism exhibits certain elitist qualities. The role of cultural capital, which was also discussed in chapter two and which plays a considerable role in alternative consumption, since a certain level of education is a crucial prerequisite, is certainly not to be underestimated in that context. Apart from that, there are other factors which reinforce the elitist image

120

of alternative consumption. Aspects like the access to information and the ability and knowledge required to interpret it, as well as the consumer's disposable income available to be spent on these goods, may be regarded as rather restrictive factors of alternative consumption. It should also be mentioned here that the geographic accessibility of ethical shopping alternatives is generally optimized for those consumers who are most likely to be willing and able to afford it. When it comes to defining the group of ethical and political consumers, however, the lack of quantitative empirical data makes it impossible to ultimately verify the statements that were made within the scope of this work. Yet, there are strong indications that alternative consumption is predominantly the realm of an educated 'elite' that not only has high levels of cultural capital but also the funds necessary to engage in alternative consumption. Therefore, Bauman's point that alternative consumption and contemporary consumer activism are essentially 'undemocratic' seems not too far-fetched after all. As the example of culture jamming has shown, activists tend to view other consumers condescendingly from a seemingly elevated position. Kozinets and Handelman term this an 'evangelical orientation.' Furthermore, the fact that culture jammers frequently propagate anti-consumption and anti-capitalism in conjunction with their proximity to anarchism contributes to a potentially undemocratic image of the movement.

Of course, consumption always has a private and individual dimension, in particular with regard to consumer choice. Any purchase decision, though socially conditioned, is first and foremost an individual decision, and thus, one can consume with the general good in mind and make one's decisions based on ethical or political considerations. This might play a role in the purchase of organic food for instance. And yet, such acts of consumption, which primarily focus on pesticide-free and genetically unmodified foods, need not necessarily have a political intention. Such choices may be considered as primarily self-interested since individual health and the health of those for whom one buys the food, like one's children, is an aspect that may carry considerable weight in decision making before reaching further political and ethical implications. This becomes slightly different as soon as other issues, such as sustainability and human rights, are involved, for then the political dimension becomes clearer, but self-interest may still play a considerable role. When it comes to market-based pressure, such as boycott participation, the political implication can hardly be denied. Yet, no matter how far political implications may reach, they seldom outweigh the consumer's self-interest. Therefore it is important to take into consideration the concept of the 'conscious consumer,' who may be well aware of the consequences of his or her consumer behavior, and who may consume ethically as long as it does not mean a radical and inconvenient change of their daily routines.

To conclude, the consumer is certainly not *the* sovereign of the market, and yet their actions might nevertheless have far-reaching consequences. The consumer's ability to exert considerable influence on the politics of the market, and thus corporate policies, by means of boycotts and buycotts has contributed to the expansion of ethical niche markets, which in turn may be seen as a result of the neoliberal segmentation of the market. The success of fair trade products, or companies like Whole Foods Market, and, to a certain extent Trader Joe's, among others of course, shows how alternative consumption in America has become a multi-billion dollar business. This may also be seen as an indication that alternative consumerism is anything but a threat to consumer capitalism, because as long as it involves consumption, and not a reduction of consumption, it may be regarded as largely following the rules of the market. Nonetheless, certain changes eventuated that may, to a considerable extent, be credited to the consumer movement. Consumers, who are not merely reactive purchasers of goods but who are also capable of producing meanings of their own, which are reflected in the choices they make, have become negotiators in the neoliberal global market. And their choice is their most powerful leverage in confronting multinational corporations with their shortcomings. In recent decades consumer activism has been making profound impacts on the corporate policies of many companies. But even though a number of corporations have discovered the benefits of corporate social responsibility, many issues of sustainability and human rights, labor conditions in cheap labor countries, or the welfare of local communities are yet to be solved. Despite the increased awareness of these issues among consumers and corporations alike, and despite the improvements in corporate policies, profound changes on national and global scales have been elusive so far.

6. Bibliography

Adbusters Media Foundation. "Blackspot Shoes | Adbusters Culturejammer Headquarters." Accessed December 10, 2012. http://www.adbusters.org/campaigns/blackspot.

–. "Buy Nothing Day + Buy Nothing Christmas #OCCUPYXMAS | Adbusters Culturejammer Headquarters." Accessed December 10, 2012. http://www.adbusters.org/campaigns/bnd.

–. "Censored TV Spots | Adbusters Culturejammer Headquarters." Accessed December 10, 2012. http://www.adbusters.org/abtv/censored_tv_spots.html.

–. "Unswooshing | Adbusters Culturejammer Headquarters." Accessed November 27, 2012. http://www.adbusters.org/spoofads/unswooshing.

Agnew, Jean-Christophe. "Coming up for Air: Consumer Culture in Historical Perspective." In *Consumer Society in American History : A Reader*, edited by Lawrence Glickman, 373–397. Ithaca, NY: Cornell University Press, 1999.

Alexander, Samuel, and Simon Ussher. "The Voluntary Simplicity Movement: A Multi-national Survey Analysis in Theoretical Context." *Journal of Consumer Culture* 12, no. 1 (March 2012): 66–86.

Anderson, Benedict. *Imagined Communities: Reflections on the Origin and Spread of Nationalism*. London; New York: Verso, 1991.

Antonio, Robert J., and Alessandro Bonnano. "A New Global Capitalism? From 'Americanism and Fordism' to 'Americanization-Globalization'." *American Studies* 41, no. 2/3 (Summer/Fall 2000): 33–77.

Axtell, James. "The First Consumer Revolution." In *Consumer Society in American History: A Reader*, edited by Lawrence Glickman, 85–99. Ithaca, NY: Cornell University Press, 1999.

Barnett, Clive, Philip Cafaro, and Terry Newholm. "Philosophy and Ethical Consumption." In *The Ethical Consumer*, edited by Rob Harrison, Terry Newholm, and Deirdre Shaw, 11–24. London: SAGE, 2005.

Baudrillard, Jean. "Consumer Society." In *Consumer Society in American History: A Reader*, edited by Lawrence Glickman, 33–56. Ithaca, NY: Cornell University Press, 1999.

–. *The System of Objects*. London; New York: Verso, 2005.

Bauman, Zygmunt. *Consuming Life*. Cambridge, UK: Polity Press, 2007.

–. *Liquid Modernity*. Repr. Cambridge, UK: Polity Press, 2001.

Billboard Liberation Front. "Billboard Liberation Front Creative Group." Accessed December 11, 2012. http://www.billboardliberation.com/clients. html.

–. "Billboard Liberation Front Creative Group." Accessed December 11, 2012. http://www.billboardliberation.com/partners.html.

Bourdieu, Pierre. *Distinction: A Social Critique of the Judgement of Taste*. London: Routledge, 2010 [1984].

Breen, T. H. *The Marketplace of Revolution: How Consumer Politics Shaped American Independence*. Oxford; New York: Oxford University Press, 2005.

–. "Baubles of Britain." *Past and Present* no. 119 (1988): 73–103.

Brooks, David. *Bobos in Paradise: The New Upper Class and How They Got There*. New York: Simon & Schuster, 2001.

Calder, Lendol. *Financing the American Dream: A Cultural History of Consumer Credit*. Princeton: Princeton University Press, 1999.

Campbell, Colin. "Considering Others and Satisfying the Self: The Moral and Ethical Dimension of Modern Consumption." In *The Moralization of the Markets*, edited by Nico Stehr, Christoph Henning, and Bernd Weiler, 213–226. New Brunswick, NJ: Transaction Publishers, 2006.

–. "Romanticism and The Consumer Ethic: Intimations of a Weber-style Thesis." *Sociological Analysis* 44, no. 4 (Winter 1983): 279–295.

–. *The Romantic Ethic and the Spirit of Modern Consumerism*. York: Alcuin Academics, 2005.

Carducci, Vince. "Culture Jamming: A Sociological Perspective." *Journal of Consumer Culture* 6, no. 1 (March 2006): 116–138.

Clark, Jr, Clifford E. "Ranch-House Suburbia: Ideals and Realities." In *Recasting America: Culture and Politics in the Age of the Cold War*, edited by Lary May, 171–191. Chicago: University of Chicago Press, 1989.

Clouder, Scott, and Rob Harrison. "The Effectiveness of Ethical Consumer Behaviour." In *The Ethical Consumer*, edited by Rob Harrison, Terry Newholm, and Deirdre Shaw, 89–104. London; Thousand Oaks, CA: SAGE, 2005.

Cohen, Lizabeth. *A Consumer's Republic: The Politics of Mass Consumption in Postwar America*. New York: Vintage Books, 2003.

–. "Encountering Mass Culture at the Grassroots: The Experience of Chicago Workers in the 1920s." *American Quarterly* 41, no. 1 (1989): 6–33.

Comstock, Sandra Curtis. "The Making of an American Icon: The Transformation of Blue Jeans During the Great Depression." In *Global Denim*, edited by Daniel Miller and Sophie Woodward, 23–50. Oxford; New York: Berg, 2011.

Crane, Andrew. "Meeting the Ethical Gaze: Challenges for Orienting to the Ethical Market." In *The Ethical Consumer*, edited by Rob Harrison, Terry Newholm, and Deirdre Shaw, 219–232. London: SAGE, 2005.

Dickinson, Roger A., and Mary L. Carsky. "The Consumer as Economic Voter." In *The Ethical Consumer*, edited by Rob Harrison, Terry Newholm, and Deirdre Shaw, 25–36. London: SAGE, 2005.

Elias, Norbert. *Die Gesellschaft der Individuen*. Frankfurt am Main: Suhrkamp, 1991.

–. *The Society of Individuals*. Translated by Michael Schröter. New York: Continuum, 2001.

Emerson, Ralph Waldo. "Ode, Inscribed to W.H. Channing. [1847]" In *The American Transcendentalists: Essential Writings*, edited by Lawrence Buell, 458–461. New York: Modern Library, 2006.

Ewen, Stuart. *Captains of Consciousness: Advertising and the Social Roots of the Consumer Culture*. New York: Basic Books, 2001 [1976].

Fair Trade Federation. *Report on Trends in the North American Fair Trade Market*. Washington, DC: Fair Trade Federation, March 2009. www.fairtradefederation.org.

Featherstone, Mike. *Consumer Culture and Postmodernism*. Los Angeles: SAGE Publications, 2007.

Federal Trade Commission. "Federal Trade Commission Resources for Reporters." Accessed November 27, 2012. http://www.ftc.gov/opa/history/timeline.shtm.

Firat, A. Fuat, and Alladi Venkatesh. "Liberatory Postmodernism and the Reenchantment of Consumption." *The Journal of Consumer Research* 22, no. 3 (1995): 239–267.

Fischer, Claude. *Made in America: A Social History of American Culture and Character*. Chicago; London: The University of Chicago Press, 2010.

Follesdal, Andreas. "Political Consumerism as Chance and Challenge." In *Politics, Products, and Markets: Exploring Political Consumerism Past and Present*, edited by Michele Micheletti, Andreas Follesdal, and Dietlind Stolle, 3–20. New Brunswick, NJ: Transaction Publishers, 2009.

Foucault, Michel. *Discipline and Punish: The Birth of the Prison*. Translated by Alan Sheridan. London: Penguin Books, 1991 [1977].

–. "The Subject and Power." In *Michel Foucault: Beyond Structuralism and Hermeneutics*, by Hubert L. Dreyfus and Paul Rabinow, 208–226. Chicago: The University of Chicago Press, 1982.

Frank, Thomas. *The Conquest of Cool: Business Culture, Counterculture, and the Rise of Hip Consumerism*. Chicago: University of Chicago Press, 1998.

Friedland, Lewis, Davan V. Shah, Nam-Jin Lee, Mark A. Rademacher, Lucy Atkinson, and Thomas Hove. "Capital, Consumption, Communication, and Citizenship: The Social Positioning of Taste and Civic Culture in the United States." *Annals of the American Academy of Political and Social Science* 611, no. 1 (May 2007): 31–50.

Gartman, David. "Postmodernism; or, the Cultural Logic of Post-Fordism?" *The Sociological Quarterly* 39, no. 1 (1998): 119–137.

GoodGuide.com. "Trader Joe's Ratings & Reviews | Best & Worst Products | GoodGuide." Accessed December 6, 2012. http://www.goodguide.com/brands/124947-trader-joes.

Gramsci, Antonio. "Americanism and Fordism." In *An Antonio Gramsci Reader: Selected Writings, 1916–1935*, edited by David Forgacs, 275–299. New York: Schocken Books, 1988.

Green America. "Greener Coffee - Green America's Responsible Shopper." *Greenamerica.org*. Accessed December 5, 2012. http://www.greenamerica.org/programs/responsibleshopper/live/coffee.cfm.

Greenberg, Cheryl. "Political Consumer Action: Some Cautionary Notes from African American History." In *Politics, Products, and Markets: Exploring Political Consumerism Past and Present*, edited by Michele Micheletti, Andreas Follesdal, and Dietlind Stolle, 63–82. New Brunswick, NJ: Transaction Publishers, 2009.

Greenpeace. "Trader Joe's Gets a Little Greener," March 29, 2010. http://www.greenpeace.org/usa/en/news-and-blogs/news/trader-joe-greener/.

Harrison, Rob, Terry Newholm, and Deirdre Shaw. *The Ethical Consumer*. London: SAGE, 2005.

Hawthorne, Fran. *Ethical Chic: The Inside Story of the Companies We Think We Love*. Boston: Beacon Press, 2012.

Heath, Joseph, and Andrew Potter. *Nation of Rebels: Why Counterculture Became Consumer Culture*. New York: HarperBusiness, 2004.

Hilton, Matthew. "Consumers and the State Since the Second World War." *Annals of the American Academy of Political and Social Science* 611 (May 2007): 66–81.

Hirsch, Fred. *Social Limits to Growth*. London: Routledge & Kegan Paul, 1976.

Holmes, Stanley. "Planet Starbucks." *Businessweek*, September 8, 2002. http://www.businessweek.com/stories/2002-09-08/planet-starbucks.

Holt, Douglas B. "Does Cultural Capital Structure American Consumption?" *The Journal of Consumer Research* 25, no. 1 (1998): 1–25.

–. "Poststructuralist Lifestyle Analysis: Conceptualizing the Social Patterning of Consumption in Postmodernity." *The Journal of Consumer Research* 23, no. 4 (1997): 326–350.

–. "Why Do Brands Cause Trouble? A Dialectical Theory of Consumer Culture and Branding." *The Journal of Consumer Research* 29, no. 1 (2002): 70–90.

Horkheimer, Max, and Theodor W. Adorno. *Dialectic of Enlightenment: Philosophical Fragments*. Stanford, CA: Stanford University Press, 2002 [1944 and 1947].

Johnston, Josée. "The Citizen-Consumer Hybrid: Ideological Tensions and the Case of Whole Foods Market." *Theory and Society* 37, no. 3 (June 2008): 229–270.

Johnston, Josée, and Michelle Szabo. "Reflexivity and the Whole Foods Market Consumer: The Lived Experience of Shopping for Change." *Agriculture and Human Values* 28, no. 3 (September 2011): 303–319.

Johnston, Josée, Michelle Szabo, and Alexandra Rodney. "Good Food, Good People: Understanding the Cultural Repertoire of Ethical Eating." *Journal of Consumer Culture* 11, no. 3 (March 18, 2011): 293–318.

Kennedy, David M. *Freedom From Fear: The American People in Depression and War, 1929–1945*. New York: Oxford University Press, 1999.

Klein, Jill Gabrielle, N. Craig Smith, and Andrew John. "Why We Boycott: Consumer Motivations for Boycott Participation." *Journal of Marketing* 68, no. 3 (July 2004): 92–109.

Klein, Naomi. *No Logo: Taking Aim at the Brand Bullies*. New York: Picador, 2002.

Kozinets, Robert V., and Jay M. Handelman. "Adversaries of Consumption: Consumer Movements, Activism, and Ideology." *Journal of Consumer Research* 31, no. 3 (December 2004): 691–704.

Lang, Tim, and Yiannis Gabriel. "A Brief History of Consumer Activism." In *The Ethical Consumer*, edited by Rob Harrison, Terry Newholm, and Deirdre Shaw, 39–53. London: SAGE, 2005.

Lasch, Christopher. *The Culture of Narcissism: American Life in an Age of Diminishing Expectations*. New York: Norton, 1991 [1979].

Lasn, Kalle. *Culture Jam: How to Reverse America's Suicidal Consumer Binge, and Why We Must*. New York: Quill, 2000.

Lears, Jackson. "A Matter of Taste: Corporate Cultural Hegemony in a Mass-Consumption Society." In *Recasting America: Culture and Politics in the Age of the Cold War*, edited by Lary May, 38–57. Chicago: University of Chicago Press, 1989.

Leinberger, Paul, and Bruce Tucker. *The New Individualists: The Generation After The Organization Man*. New York, NY: HarperCollins, 1991.

Leone, Richard C. "Public Interest Advocacy and the Regulatory Process." *The Annals of the American Academy of Political and Social Science* 400, no. 1 (1972): 46–58.

Lipsitz, George. "Land of a Thousand Dances: Youth, Minorities, and the Rise of Rock and Roll." In *Recasting America: Culture and Politics in the Age of the Cold War*, edited by Lary May, 267–284. Chicago: University of Chicago Press, 1989.

Loeb, Walter. "Aldi's Trader Joe's Is a Winner." *Forbes.com*, May 17, 2012. http://www.forbes.com/sites/walterloeb/2012/05/17/aldis-trader-joes-is-a-winner/3/.

MacDonald, Christine. "The Big Green Buyout: Countless Green Brands Have Been Snapped Up By Big Corporations." *E - The Environmental Magazine*, August 2011.

Mahler, Daniel, Jeremy Barker, Louis Belsand, and Otto Schulz. *Green Winners: The Performance of Sustainability-focused Companies During the Financial Crisis*. Chicago: A.T. KEARNEY, 2009. http://www.atkearney.com/de/paper/-/asset_publisher/dVxv4Hz2h8bS/content/green-winners/10192.

Marcuse, Herbert. *One-Dimensional Man: Studies in the Ideology of Advanced Industrial Society*. London: Routledge, 2002 [1964].

McCracken, Grant. *Culture and Consumption II: Markets, Meaning, and Brand Management*. Bloomington: Indiana University Press, 2005.

–. *Culture and Consumption: New Approaches to the Symbolic Character of Consumer Goods and Activities*. Bloomington: Indiana University Press, 1990.

–. *Transformations: Identity Construction in Contemporary Culture*. Bloomington: Indiana University Press, 2008.

Micheletti, Michele. *Political Virtue and Shopping: Individuals, Consumerism, and Collective Action*. Basingstoke, UK: Palgrave Macmillan, 2010.

–. "Why More Women? Issues of Gender and Political Consumerism." In *Politics, Products, and Markets: Exploring Political Consumerism Past and Present*, 245–264. New Brunswick, NJ: Transaction Publishers, 2009.

Miles, Steven. *Consumerism: As a Way of Life*. London; Thousand Oaks, CA: Sage Publications, 1998.

Miller, Daniel. *Consumption and its Consequences*. Cambridge: Polity, 2012.

Mills, C. Wright. *The Sociological Imagination*. New York: Oxford University Press, 1959.

Moorhouse, H. F. "The 'Work' Ethic and 'Leisure' Activity: The Hot Rod in Post-War America." In *Consumer Society in American History: A Reader*, edited by Lawrence Glickman, 277–297. Ithaca, NY: Cornell University Press, 1999.

Muniz, Albert M., and Thomas C. O'Guinn. "Brand Community." *The Journal of Consumer Research* 27, no. 4 (2001): 412–432.

Murray, Jeff B., and Julie L. Ozanne. "The Critical Imagination: Emancipatory Interests in Consumer Research." *The Journal of Consumer Research* 18, no. 2 (1991): 129–144.

Nader, Ralph. "Taming the Corporate Tiger [1966]." In *The Ralph Nader Reader*, edited by Ralph Nader and Barbara Ehrenreich, 133–144. New York: Seven Stories, 2000.

–. "The Safe Car You Can't Buy [1959]." In *The Ralph Nader Reader*, edited by Ralph Nader and Barbara Ehrenreich, 266–272. New York: Seven Stories, 2000.

Nader.org. "Biographical Facts | The Nader Page." Accessed November 29, 2012. http://nader.org/2006/03/01/biographical-facts/.

Neilson, Lisa A., and Pamela Paxton. "Social Capital and Political Consumerism: A Multilevel Analysis." *Social Problems* 57, no. 1 (February 2010): 5–24.

Nelson, Michelle, Mark A. Rademacher, and Hye-Jin Paek. "Downshifting Consumer = Upshifting Citizen? An Examination of a Local Freecycle Community." *Annals of the American Academy of Political and Social Science* 611 (May 2007): 141–156.

Nietzsche, Friedrich. *Daybreak: Thoughts on the Prejudices of Morality*. Edited by Maudemarie Clark and Brian Leiter. Translated by R. J Hollingdale. Cambridge: Cambridge University Press, 1997.

Ollman, Bertell. "Market Mystification in Capitalism and Market Socialist Societies." In *Market Socialism*, edited by Bertell Ollman, 81–122.

New York: Routledge, 1998. Quoted in: Harrison, Rob, Terry Newholm, and Deirdre Shaw. *The Ethical Consumer*. London: SAGE, 2005.

Packard, Vance. *The Waste Makers*. Brooklyn: ig Publishing, 2011.

Patterson, James T. *Grand Expectations: Postwar America, 1945–1974*. New York: Oxford University Press, 1996.

–. *Restless Giant: The United States from Watergate to Bush v. Gore*. New York: Oxford University Press, 2005.

Pepper, Miriam, Tim Jackson, and David Uzzell. "An Examination of the Values That Motivate Socially Conscious and Frugal Consumer Behaviors." *International Journal of Consumer Studies* 33, no. 2 (2009): 126–136.

Peretti, Jonah, and Michele Micheletti. "The Nike Sweatshop Email: Political Consumerism, Internet, and Culture Jamming." In *Politics, Products, and Markets: Exploring Political Consumerism Past and Present*, edited by Michele Micheletti, Andreas Follesdal, and Dietlind Stolle, 127–142. New Brunswick, NJ: Transaction Publishers, 2009.

Pollan, Michael. *The Omnivore's Dilemma: A Natural History of Four Meals*. New York: Penguin Press, 2006.

Portwood-Stacer, Laura. "Anti-consumption as Tactical Resistance: Anarchists, Subculture, and Activist Strategy." *Journal of Consumer Culture* 12, no. 1 (March 2012): 82–105.

Potter, David M. *People of Plenty: Economic Abundance and the American Character*. Chicago: The University of Chicago Press, 1954.

Public Citizen. "About Public Citizen." Accessed November 29, 2012. http://www.citizen.org/Page.aspx?pid=2306.

–. "Public Citizen Accomplishments." Accessed November 28, 2012. http://www.citizen.org/Page.aspx?pid=2307.

–. "Public Citizen Home Page." Accessed November 29, 2012. http://www.citizen.org/Page.aspx?pid=183.

Riesman, David, Nathan Glazer, and Reuel Denney. *The Lonely Crowd: A study of the Changing American Character*. Reprint. New Haven, CT: Yale University Press, 2001 [1961].

Roszak, Theodore. *The Making of a Counter Culture : Reflections on the Technocratic Society and Its Youthful Opposition.* Berkeley: University of California Press, 1995.

Sandlin, Jennifer A., and Jamie L. Callahan. "Deviance, Dissonance, and Détournement." *Journal of Consumer Culture* 9, no. 1 (March 2009): 79–115.

Schor, Juliet B. "In Defense of Consumer Critique: Revisiting the Consumption Debates of the Twentieth Century." *Annals of the American Academy of Political and Social Science* 611 (May 2007): 16–30.

Schudson, Michael. "Citizens, Consumers, and the Good Society." *Annals of the American Academy of Political and Social Science* 611 (May 2007): 236–249.

–. "The Troubling Equivalence of Citizen and Consumer." *Annals of the American Academy of Political and Social Science* 608 (November 2006): 193–204.

Sennett, Richard. *The Fall of Public Man.* New York: Norton, 1992 [1974].

Shah, Davan V., Douglas M. McLeod, Eungkyung Kim, Sun Young Lee, Melissa R. Gotlieb, Shirley S. Ho, and Hilde Breivik. "Political Consumerism: How Communication and Consumption Orientations Drive 'Lifestyle Politics'." *Annals of the American Academy of Political and Social Science* 611 (May 2007): 217–235.

Simmel, Georg. "Fashion." *American Journal of Sociology* 62, no. 6 (May 1957): 541–558.

Simon, Bryant. "Not Going to Starbucks: Boycotts and the Out-Sourcing of Politics in the Branded World." *Journal of Consumer Culture* 11, no. 2 (July 2011): 145–167.

Slater, Don. *Consumer Culture and Modernity.* Cambridge, UK; Cambridge, MA: Polity Press; Blackwell Publishers, 1997.

Smith, Jacquelyn. "America's Most Trustworthy Companies." *Forbes.com*, March 20, 2012. http://www.forbes.com/sites/jacquelynsmith/2012/03/20/americas-most-trustworthy-companies/2/.

–. "The World's Most Ethical Companies." *Forbes.com*, March 15, 2011. http://www.forbes.com/2011/03/15/most-ethical-companies-leadership-responsibility-ethisphere.html.

Starbucks. "Responsibly Grown and Fair Trade Coffee." Accessed December 5, 2012. http://www.starbucks.com/responsibility/sourcing/coffee.

Stolle, Dietlind, and Marc Hooghe. "Consumers as Political Participants?" In *Politics, Products, and Markets: Exploring Political Consumerism Past and Present*, edited by Michele Micheletti, Andreas Follesdal, and Dietlind Stolle, 265–288. New Brunswick, NJ: Transaction Publishers, 2009.

Stolle, Dietlind, Marc Hooghe, and Michele Micheletti. "Politics in the Supermarket: Political Consumerism as a Form of Political Participation." *International Political Sciene Review* 26, no. 3 (July 2005): 245–269.

Stone, Gregory P. "City Shoppers and Urban Identification: Observations on the Social Psychology of City Life." *American Journal of Sociology* 60, no. 1 (July 1954): 36–45.

Storey, John. *Cultural Consumption and Everyday Life*. London: Arnold, 1999.

Sullivan, Patricia A., and Steven R. Goldzwig. "Ralph Nader: Consumer Advocate, Lawyer, Presidential Candidate." In *American Voices: An Encyclopedia of Contemporary Orators*, edited by Bernard K. Duffy and Richard W. Leeman, 330–338. Westport, CT: Greenwood Press, 2005.

Szmigin, Isabelle, Marylyn Carrigan, and Morven G. McEachern. "The Conscious Consumer: Taking a Flexible Approach to Ethical Behaviour." *International Journal of Consumer Studies* 33, no. 2 (March 2009): 224–231.

Trader Joe's. "Customer Updates." Accessed December 5, 2012. http://www.traderjoes.com/about/customer-updates-responses.asp?i=80.

–. "Neighborhood Involvement" Trader Joe's. Accessed December 5, 2012. http://www.traderjoes.com/stores/neighborhood-involvement.asp.

U.S Library of Congress, Congressional Research Service. *The Dodd-Frank Wall Street Reform and Consumer Protection Act: Regulations to Be Issued by the Consumer Financial Protection Bureau* By Curtis W. Copeland, CRS Report R41380. Washington, DC: Office of Congressional Information and Publishing, August 25, 2010.

Veblen, Thorstein. *The Theory of the Leisure Class*. New York: Dover Publications, 1994.

Vogel, David. "Tracing the American Roots of the Political Consumerism Movement." In *Politics, Products, and Markets: Exploring Political Consumerism Past and Present*, edited by Michele Micheletti, Andreas Follesdal, and Dietlind Stolle, 83–100. New Brunswick, NJ: Transaction Publishers, 2009.

Whole Foods Market. "Green Mission." Accessed December 5, 2012. http://www.wholefoodsmarket.com/mission-values/environmental-stewardship/green-mission.